W9-BUL-307

The Gospel of Mark

Avriana Surdich

Presented to

Sami Shaker

Presented by

6/20/2023

Date

Completing Alpha Course

Occasion

God Bless you!

The Gospel of Mark
The Illustrated International Children's Bible®

icb
International
Children's Bible

Illustrations by Keith Neely and David Miles

The preliminary research and development of the International Children's Bible® was done by the World Bible Translation Center, Inc., Fort Worth, TX 76182

Printed in the United States of America

1 2 3 4 5 6 7 8 9 10 - 13 12 11 10 09 08 07 06

The
Gospel
of
Mark

icb
The Illustrated
International Children's Bible®

Design and Illustration from
Neely Publishing LLC.

Individual contributors:
Keith R. Neely, David Miles, Roberta Neely,
Bridget Harlow and Thomas R. Zuber

Tommy
NELSON

A Division of Thomas Nelson Publishers
Since 1798

www.TommyNelson.com
a division of
Thomas Nelson, Inc.
www.thomasnelson.com

Introduction

Welcome! You've just picked up one of the most amazing books of all time, the Holy Bible. This book of the Bible, Mark, is presented in a way that has never been done before. Want to know how and why we've done it this way? Keep reading to find out!

Our Purpose

We did not want to create just another children's Bible storybook. In other words, we didn't want to have Bible pictures alongside words that are a retelling of God's Word, the Holy Scriptures. We wanted to draw attention to, magnify, and clarify the actual Word of God. In those words lies the power to change the lives of children and adults alike!

"God's word is alive and working." Hebrews 4:12

"But the word of the Lord will live forever." 1 Peter 1:25

In the same way that written illustrations or "word pictures" are used to help make an idea easy to understand and memorable, our visual illustrations will make the actual Word of God easier to understand than ever before.

The Illustrated International Children's Bible®

The International Children's Bible® was the first translation created especially for children. It has been illustrated in a frame-by-frame format style. These realistic images help illustrate the actual Scriptures . . . the events of the Bible. The format helps to carry the reader easily through each story like a visual movie. This not only makes the verses easier to understand, but also easier to memorize!

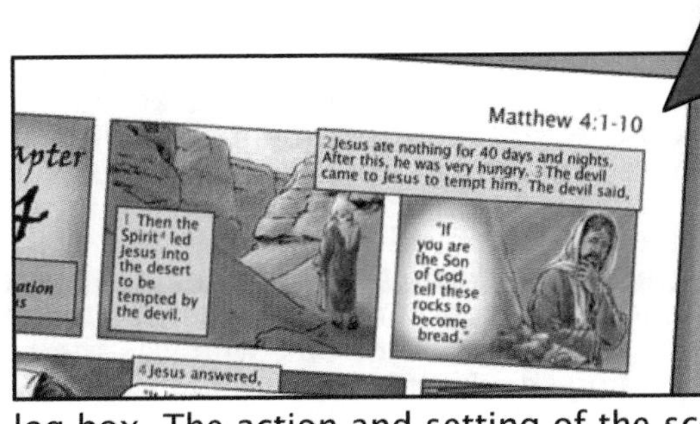
Matthew 4:1-10
2 Jesus ate nothing for 40 days and nights. After this, he was very hungry. 3 The devil came to Jesus to tempt him. The devil said,
1 Then the Spirit[d] led Jesus into the desert to be tempted by the devil.
"If you are the Son of God, tell these rocks to become bread."
4 Jesus answered,

Actual Scriptures: Yes, that's right . . . the pages of this book are actual Bible verses. On some pages you'll see the characters speaking by the use of a dialog box. The action and setting of the scene is readily apparent by the backgrounds. What a great way to read and learn your Bible! Some of the verses are not a person speaking, so they will be in plain boxes. You might see some small "d's" in the text. These indicate a word that will have a definition in the dictionary found at the back of full ICB Bibles.

Old Testament quotations are shown in a separate treatment. They are in a parchment like background to represent that they are older words, almost like a treasured antique. They will usually have the book, chapter, and verse with them so you can know where they came from in the Old Testament.

5 "Tell the people of Jerusalem, 'Your king is coming to you. He is gentle and riding on a donkey. He is on the colt of a donkey.' "

Zechariah 9:9

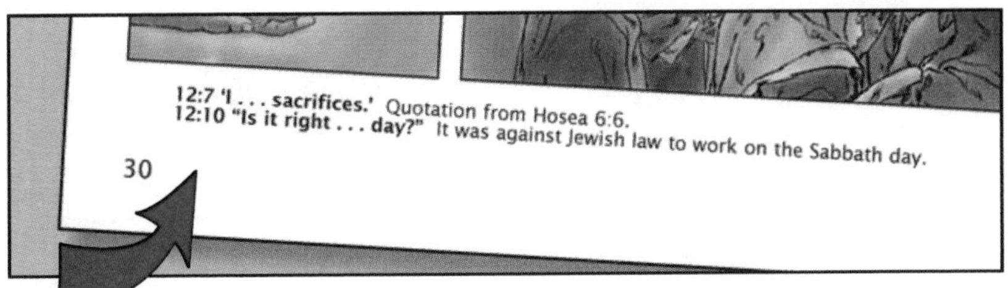
12:7 'I . . . sacrifices.' Quotation from Hosea 6:6.
12:10 "Is it right . . . day?" It was against Jewish law to work on the Sabbath day.
30

Footnotes appear at the bottom of some pages. They are represented in the Bible verses by a small "n." That will let you know that there is a note at the bottom of the page that gives you a little more information about that word or phrase. Just more information that's helpful to know!

In some chapters and verses there will not be a lot of interaction between Bible characters, but you will see background scenery, maps, and other interesting treatments to help make your Bible reading more fun and helpful. Most Bible storybooks are just that . . . stories retold to make them easier to understand. Never before has actual Bible Scripture been illustrated in this form so that children and adults can immediately read and know what is going on in a certain verse–who was talking, what time of day it was, was it inside or out, who was there. We hope you enjoy reading this Bible and have fun learning along the way!

The Publishers

Look for these other titles...

The Acts of the Apostles
The Illustrated International Children's Bible

The Gospel of John
The Illustrated International Children's Bible

The Gospel of Matthew
The Illustrated International Children's Bible

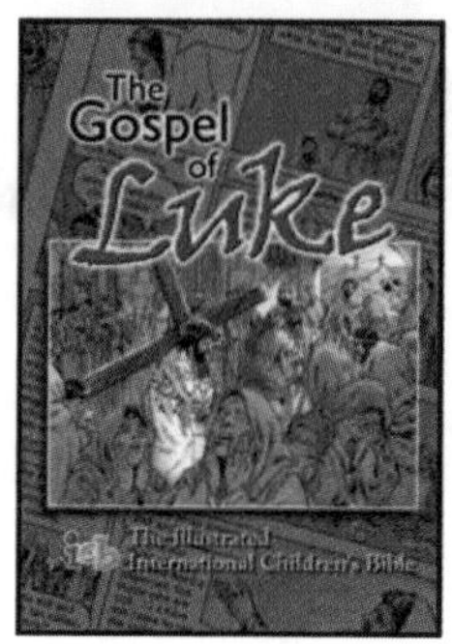
The Gospel of Luke
The Illustrated International Children's Bible

and

icb International Children's Bible
The New Testament

Table of Contents

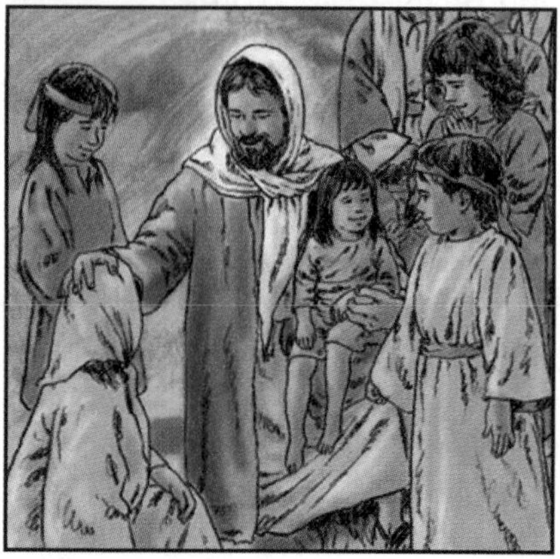

The Gospel of Mark

Mark Chapter 1
John Prepares for Jesus
1 This is the beginning of the Good
News[d] about Jesus Christ, the Son of
God,[n] 2 as the prophet[d] Isaiah
wrote:
"I will send my
messenger ahead
of you. He will prepare
your way."
Malachi 3:1
3 "There is a voice of a
man who calls out in
the desert: 'Prepare
the way for the Lord.
Make the road straight
for him.' "
Isaiah 40:3
4 John was baptizing people in the
desert. He preached a baptism of
changed hearts and lives for the for-
giveness of sins. 5 All the people
from Judea and Jerusalem were
going out to John. They told about
the sins they had done. Then they
were baptized by him in the Jordan
River. 6 John wore clothes made
from camel's hair and had a leather
belt around his waist. He ate
locusts[d] and wild honey. 7 This is
what John preached to the people:
"There is one coming later
who is greater than I. I am not
good enough even to kneel
down and untie his sandals. 8 I
baptize you with water. But the
one who is coming will baptize
you with the Holy Spirit."[d]

1:1 the Son of God Some Greek copies do not have this phrase.

Jesus Is Baptized

9 At that time Jesus came from the town of Nazareth in Galilee to the place where John was. John baptized Jesus in the Jordan River.
10 When Jesus was coming up out of the water, he saw heaven open. The Holy Spirit[d] came down on him like a dove.

11 A voice came from heaven and said:

"You are my Son and I love you. I am very pleased with you."

12 Then the Spirit sent Jesus into the desert alone.

13 He was in the desert 40 days and was there with the wild animals. While he was in the desert, he was tempted by Satan. Then angels came and took care of Jesus.

Jesus Chooses Some Followers

14 After John was put in prison, Jesus went into Galilee and preached the Good News[d] from God.
15 Jesus said,

"The right time has come. The kingdom of God is near. Change your hearts and lives and believe the Good News!"

16 When Jesus was walking by Lake Galilee, he saw Simon[n] and Simon's brother, Andrew. They were fishermen and were throwing a net into the lake to catch fish.
17 Jesus said to them,

"Come and follow me. I will make you fishermen for men."

18 So Simon and Andrew immediately left their nets and followed him.
19 Jesus continued walking by Lake Galilee. He saw two more brothers, James and John, the sons of Zebedee. They were in their boat, preparing their nets to catch fish.
20 Their father Zebedee and the men who worked for him were in the boat with the brothers. When Jesus saw the brothers, he called them to come with him. They left their father and followed Jesus.

1:16 Simon Simon's other name was Peter.

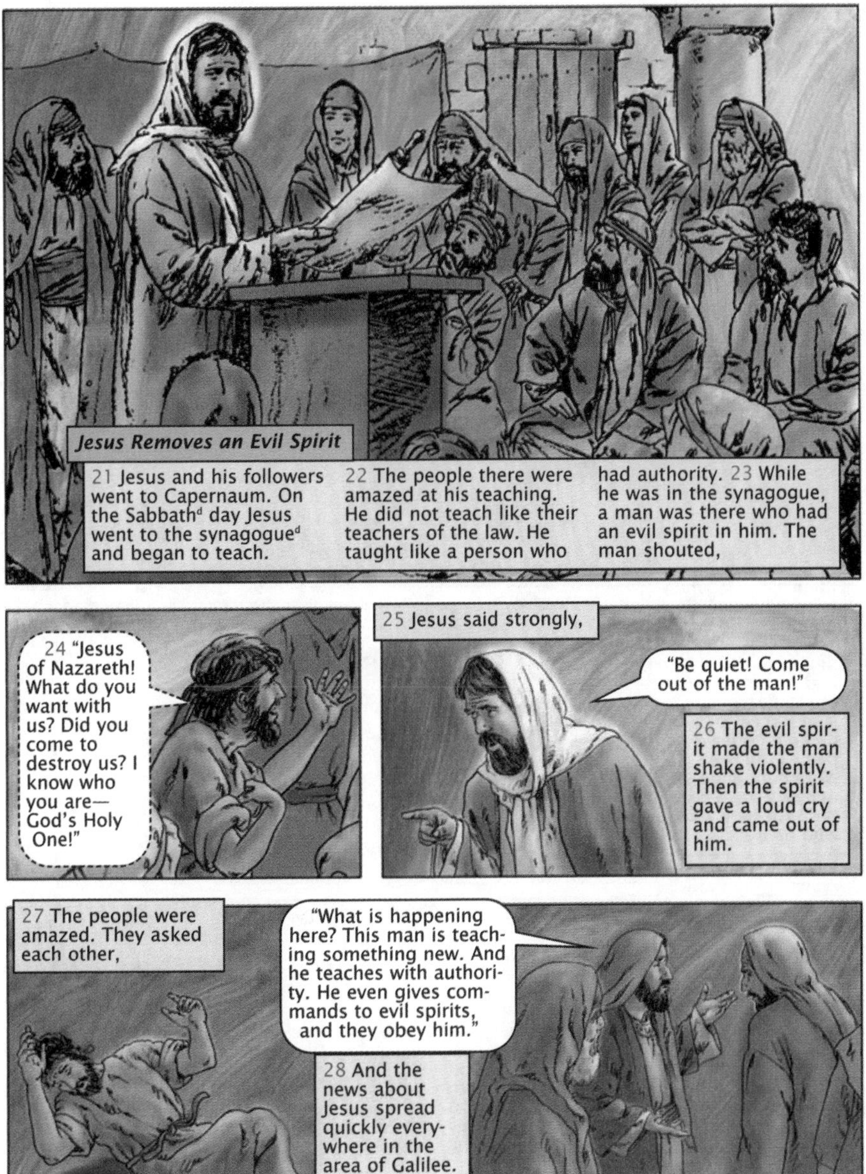

Jesus Removes an Evil Spirit

21 Jesus and his followers
went to Capernaum. On
the Sabbath[d] day Jesus
went to the synagogue[d]
and began to teach.
22 The people there were
amazed at his teaching.
He did not teach like their
teachers of the law. He
taught like a person who
had authority. 23 While
he was in the synagogue,
a man was there who had
an evil spirit in him. The
man shouted,

24 "Jesus of Nazareth! What do you want with us? Did you come to destroy us? I know who you are—God's Holy One!"

25 Jesus said strongly,
"Be quiet! Come out of the man!"
26 The evil spirit made the man shake violently. Then the spirit gave a loud cry and came out of him.

27 The people were amazed. They asked each other,
"What is happening here? This man is teaching something new. And he teaches with authority. He even gives commands to evil spirits, and they obey him."
28 And the news about Jesus spread quickly everywhere in the area of Galilee.

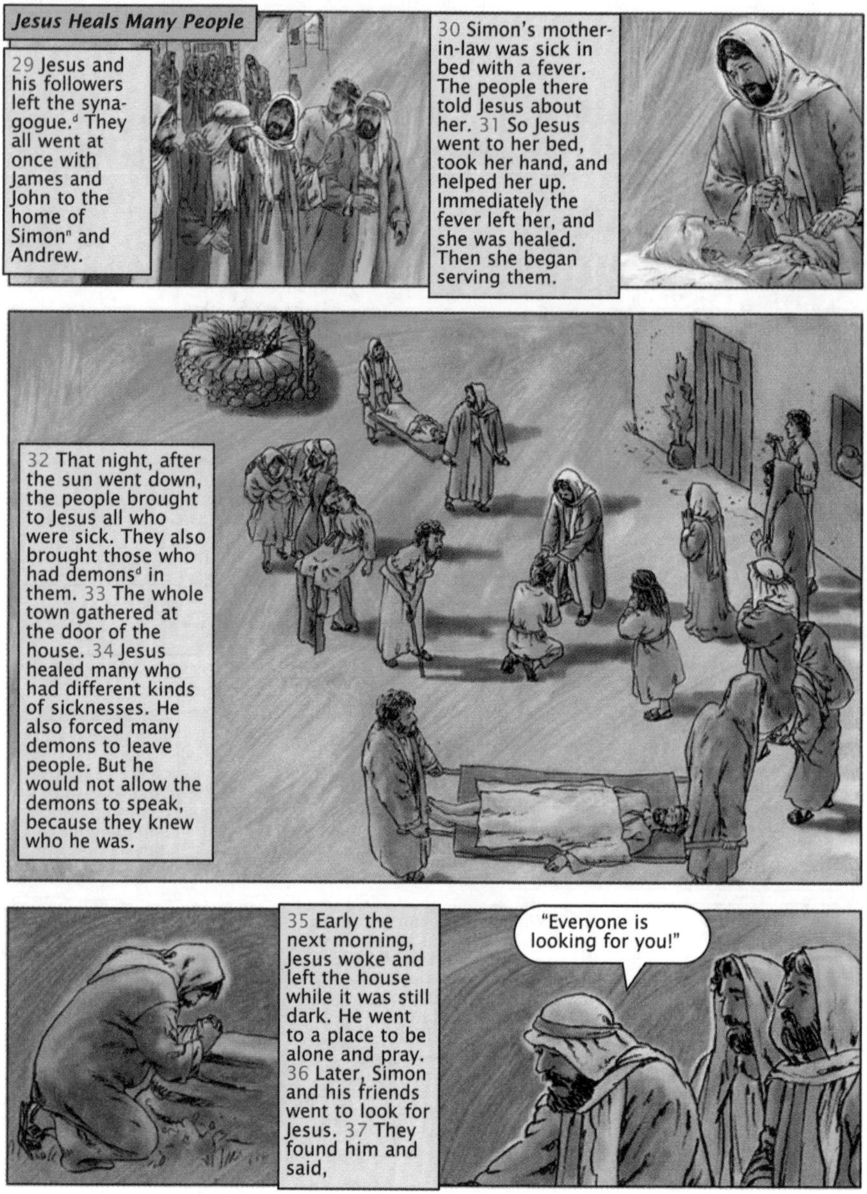

Jesus Heals Many People

29 Jesus and
his followers
left the syna-
gogue.[d] They
all went at
once with
James and
John to the
home of
Simon[n] and
Andrew.

30 Simon's mother-
in-law was sick in
bed with a fever.
The people there
told Jesus about
her. 31 So Jesus
went to her bed,
took her hand, and
helped her up.
Immediately the
fever left her, and
she was healed.
Then she began
serving them.

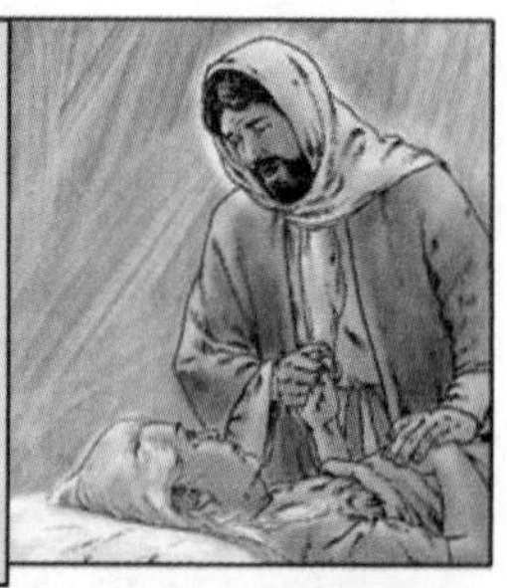

32 That night, after
the sun went down,
the people brought
to Jesus all who
were sick. They also
brought those who
had demons[d] in
them. 33 The whole
town gathered at
the door of the
house. 34 Jesus
healed many who
had different kinds
of sicknesses. He
also forced many
demons to leave
people. But he
would not allow the
demons to speak,
because they knew
who he was.

35 Early the
next morning,
Jesus woke and
left the house
while it was still
dark. He went
to a place to be
alone and pray.
36 Later, Simon
and his friends
went to look for
Jesus. 37 They
found him and
said,

"Everyone is looking for you!"

1:29 Simon Simon's other name was Peter.

38 Jesus answered,
"We should go somewhere else, to other towns around here. Then I can preach there too. That is the reason I came."
39 So he traveled everywhere in Galilee. He preached in the synagogues and forced demons to leave people.

Jesus Heals a Sick Man
40 A man who had a harmful skin disease came to Jesus. The man fell to his knees and begged Jesus,
"I know that you can heal me if you will."

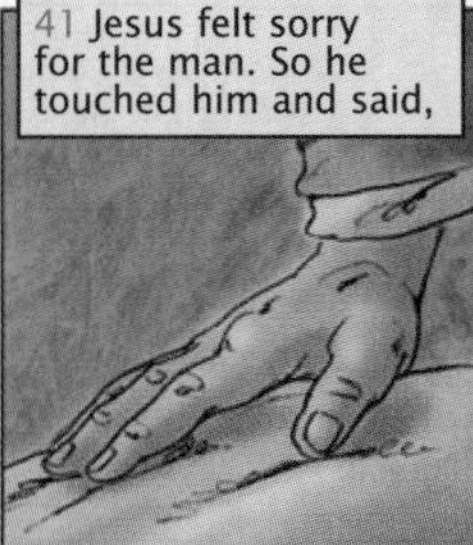
41 Jesus felt sorry for the man. So he touched him and said,

"I want to heal you. Be healed!"

42 At once the disease left the man, and he was healed. 43 Jesus told the man to go at once. But Jesus warned him strongly,
44 "Don't tell anyone about what I did for you. But go and show yourself to the priest. And offer a gift to God because you have been healed. Offer the gift that Moses commanded.[n] This will show the people that you are healed."
45 The man left there, but he told everyone he saw that Jesus had healed him. So the news about Jesus spread. That is the reason Jesus could not enter a town if people saw him. He stayed in places where nobody lived. But people came from all the towns to wherever he was.

Chapter 2
Jesus Heals a Paralyzed Man

1 A few days later, Jesus came back to Capernaum. The news spread that he was home. 2 So many people gathered to hear him preach that the house was full. There was no place to stand, not even outside the door. Jesus was teaching them.

1:44 Moses commanded Read about this in Leviticus 14:1-32.

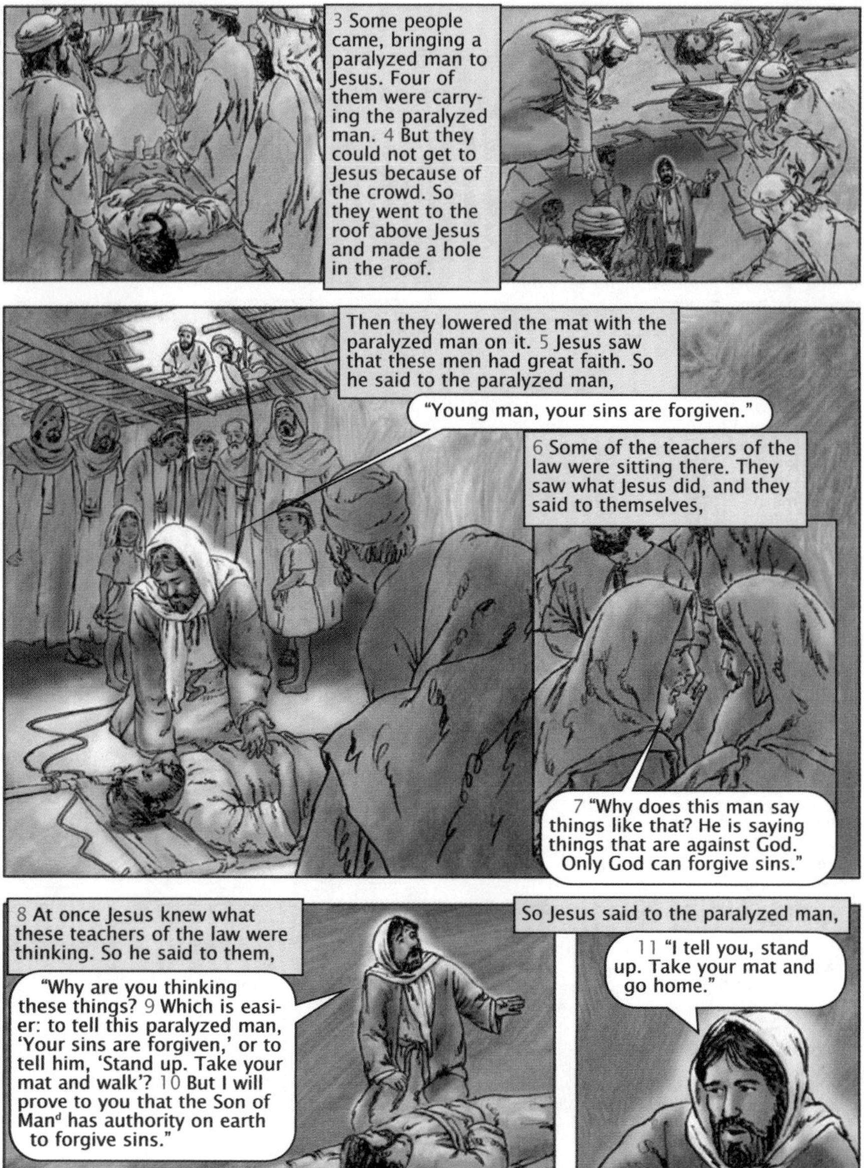

3 Some people came, bringing a paralyzed man to Jesus. Four of them were carrying the paralyzed man. 4 But they could not get to Jesus because of the crowd. So they went to the roof above Jesus and made a hole in the roof.

Then they lowered the mat with the paralyzed man on it. 5 Jesus saw that these men had great faith. So he said to the paralyzed man,

"Young man, your sins are forgiven."

6 Some of the teachers of the law were sitting there. They saw what Jesus did, and they said to themselves,

7 "Why does this man say things like that? He is saying things that are against God. Only God can forgive sins."

8 At once Jesus knew what these teachers of the law were thinking. So he said to them,

"Why are you thinking these things? 9 Which is easier: to tell this paralyzed man, 'Your sins are forgiven,' or to tell him, 'Stand up. Take your mat and walk'? 10 But I will prove to you that the Son of Man[d] has authority on earth to forgive sins."

So Jesus said to the paralyzed man,

11 "I tell you, stand up. Take your mat and go home."

12 Immediately the paralyzed man stood up. He took his mat and walked out while everyone was watching him.
The people were amazed and praised God. They said,

"We have never seen anything like this!"

13 Jesus went to the lake again. A crowd followed him there, and he taught them.

14 While he was walking beside the lake, he saw a tax collector named Levi son of Alphaeus. Levi was sitting in the tax office. Jesus said to him,

"Follow me."

And Levi stood up and followed Jesus.

15 Later that day, Jesus ate at Levi's house. There were many tax collectors and "sinners" eating there with Jesus and his followers. Many people like this followed Jesus.

16 The teachers of the law who were Pharisees[d] saw Jesus eating with the tax collectors and "sinners." They asked his followers,

"Why does he eat with tax collectors and sinners?"

17 Jesus heard this and said to them,

"Healthy people don't need a doctor. It is the sick who need a doctor. I did not come to invite good people. I came to invite sinners."

Jesus' Followers Are Criticized

18 One day the followers of John[n] and the Pharisees[d] were giving up eating.[n] Some people came to Jesus and said,

"John's followers and the followers of the Pharisees give up eating. But your followers don't. Why?"

19 Jesus answered,

"When there is a wedding, the friends of the bridegroom are not sad while he is with them. They do not give up eating while the bridegroom is still there.

20 But the time will come when the bridegroom will leave them. Then the friends will be sad and will give up eating.

21 "When a person sews a patch over a hole on an old coat, he never uses a piece

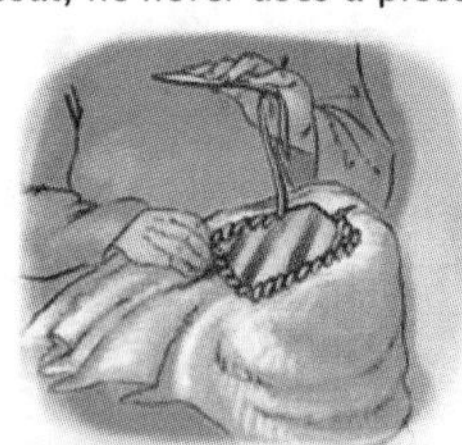

of cloth that is not yet shrunk. If he does, the patch will shrink and pull away from the coat. Then the hole will be worse.

22 Also, no one ever pours new wine into old leather

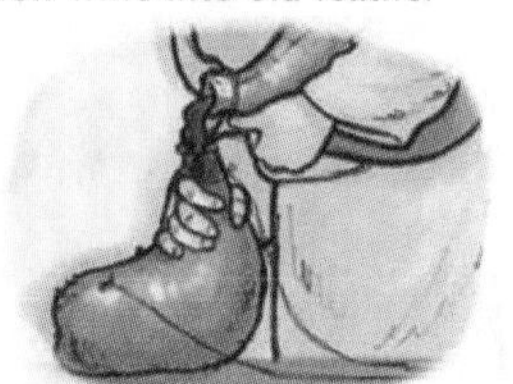

bags for holding wine. If he does, the new wine will break the bags, and the wine will be ruined along with the bags for the wine. People

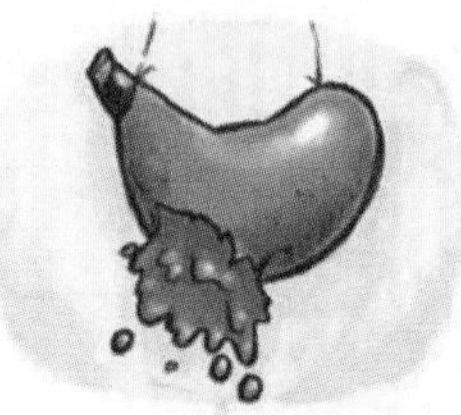

always put new wine into new leather bags."

2:18 John John the Baptist who preached to the Jews about Christ's coming (Mark 1:4-8).
2:18 giving up eating This is called "fasting." The people would give up eating for a special time of prayer and worship to God. It was also done to show sadness.

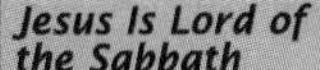

Jesus Is Lord of the Sabbath

23 On the Sabbath[d] day, Jesus was walking through some grainfields. His followers were with him and picked some grain to eat.

24 The Pharisees[d] saw this and said to Jesus,

"Why are your followers doing what is not lawful on the Sabbath?"

25 Jesus answered,

"You have read what David did when he and those with him were hungry and needed food. 26 It was during the time of Abiathar the high priest. David went into God's house and ate the bread that was made holy for God. The law of Moses says that only priests may eat that bread. But David also gave some of the bread to those who were with him."

27 Then Jesus said to the Pharisees,

"The Sabbath day was made to help people. They were not made to be ruled by the Sabbath day. 28 The Son of Man[d] is Lord even of the Sabbath."

Chapter 3

Jesus Heals a Man's Crippled Hand

1 Another time when Jesus went into a synagogue,[d] a man with a crippled hand was there. 2 Some people there wanted to see Jesus do something wrong so they could accuse him. They watched him closely to see if he would heal the man on the Sabbath[d] day. 3 Jesus said to the man with the crippled hand,

"Stand up here in front of everyone."

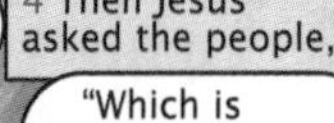

4 Then Jesus asked the people,

"Which is right on the Sabbath day: to do good, or to do evil? Is it right to save a life or to destroy one?"

But they said nothing to answer him.

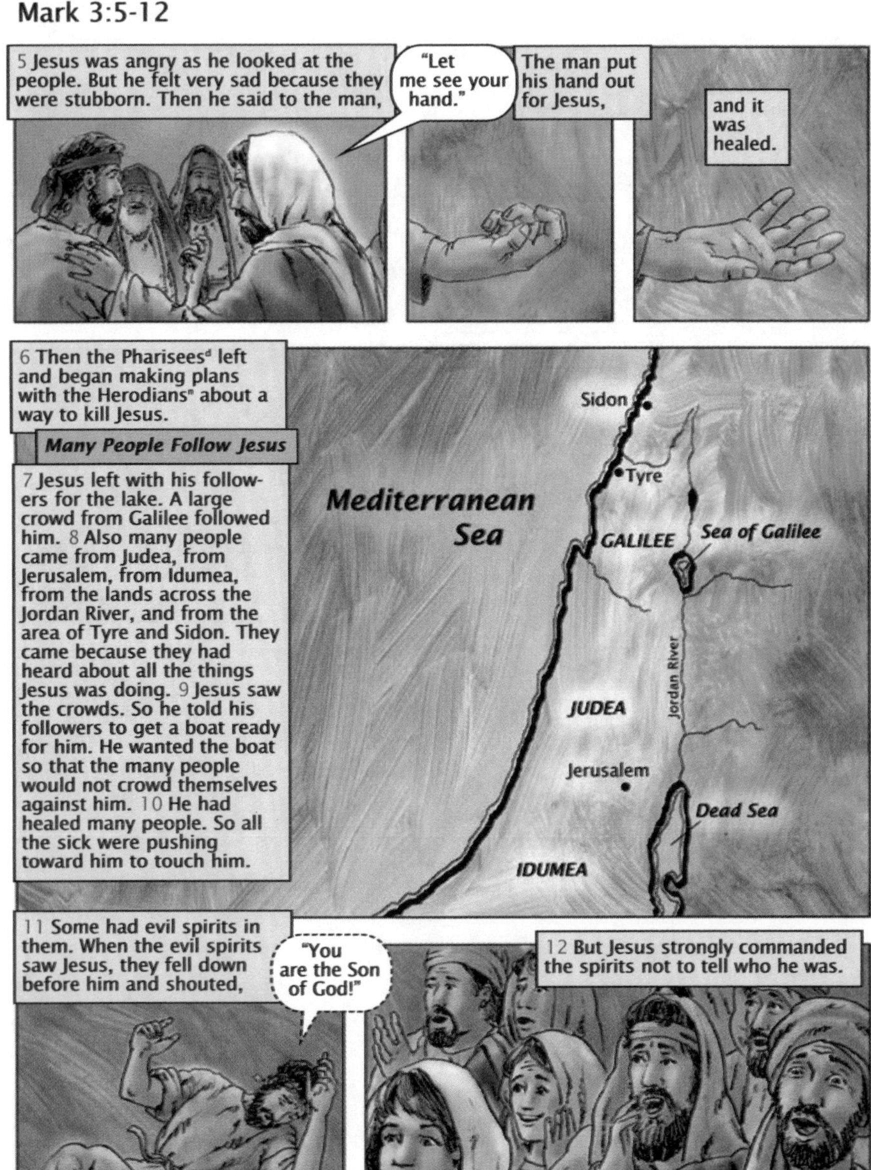
5 Jesus was angry as he looked at the people. But he felt very sad because they were stubborn. Then he said to the man,
"Let me see your hand."
The man put his hand out for Jesus,
and it was healed.
6 Then the Pharisees[d] left and began making plans with the Herodians* about a way to kill Jesus.
Many People Follow Jesus
7 Jesus left with his followers for the lake. A large crowd from Galilee followed him. 8 Also many people came from Judea, from Jerusalem, from Idumea, from the lands across the Jordan River, and from the area of Tyre and Sidon. They came because they had heard about all the things Jesus was doing. 9 Jesus saw the crowds. So he told his followers to get a boat ready for him. He wanted the boat so that the many people would not crowd themselves against him. 10 He had healed many people. So all the sick were pushing toward him to touch him.
Sidon
Tyre
Mediterranean Sea
GALILEE
Sea of Galilee
Jordan River
JUDEA
Jerusalem
Dead Sea
IDUMEA
11 Some had evil spirits in them. When the evil spirits saw Jesus, they fell down before him and shouted,
"You are the Son of God!"
12 But Jesus strongly commanded the spirits not to tell who he was.

3:6 Herodians A political group that followed Herod and his family.

Jesus Chooses His 12 Apostles

13 Then Jesus went up on a
hill and called some men to
come to him. These were the
men Jesus wanted, and they
went up to him. 14 Jesus
chose 12 men and called
them apostles.[nd] He wanted
these 12 to be with him, and
he wanted to send them to
other places to preach.
15 He also wanted them to
have the power to force
demons[d] out of people.
16 These are the 12 men he
chose: Simon (Jesus gave
him the name Peter);
17 James and John, the sons
of Zebedee (Jesus gave them
the name Boanerges, which
means "Sons of Thunder");
18 Andrew, Philip, Barthol-
omew, Matthew, Thomas,
James the son of Alphaeus,
Thaddaeus, Simon the
Zealot,[d] 19 and Judas
Iscariot. Judas is the one who
gave Jesus to his enemies.

People Say Jesus Has a Devil

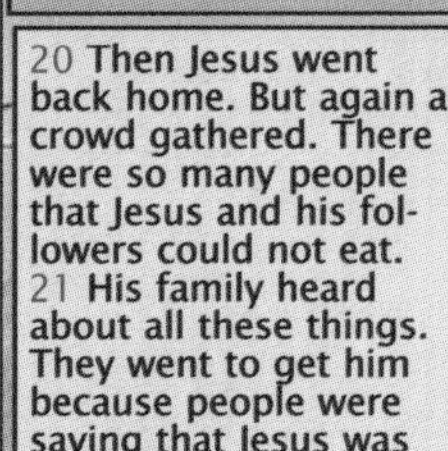
20 Then Jesus went
back home. But again a
crowd gathered. There
were so many people
that Jesus and his fol-
lowers could not eat.
21 His family heard
about all these things.
They went to get him
because people were
saying that Jesus was
out of his mind.

3:14 and called them apostles Some Greek copies do not have this phrase.

22 And the teachers of the law from Jerusalem were saying,
"Beelzebul[d] is living inside him!
He uses power from the ruler of demons[d] to force demons out."
23 So Jesus called the people together and used stories to teach them. He said,
"Satan will not force his own demons out of people. 24 A kingdom that fights against itself cannot continue. 25 And a family that is divided cannot continue. 26 And if Satan is against himself and fights against his own people, then he cannot continue. And that is the end of Satan. 27 If a person wants to enter a strong man's house and steal his things, first he must tie up the strong man. Then the thief can steal the things from the strong man's house. 28 I tell you the truth. All sins that people do can be forgiven. And all the bad things people say against God can be forgiven. 29 But any person who says bad things against the Holy Spirit[d] will never be forgiven. He is guilty of a sin that continues forever."
30 Jesus said this because the teachers of the law said that Jesus had an evil spirit inside him.
Jesus' True Family
31 Then Jesus' mother and brothers arrived. They stood outside and sent someone in to tell him to come out. 32 Many people were sitting around Jesus. They said to him,
"Your mother and brothers[n] are waiting for you outside."
33 Jesus asked,
"Who is my mother? Who are my brothers?"

3:32 brothers Some Greek copies continue, "and sisters."

34 Then Jesus looked at those
sitting around him. He said,
"Here are my
mother and my
brothers! 35 My
true brother and
sister and mother
are those who do
the things God
wants."

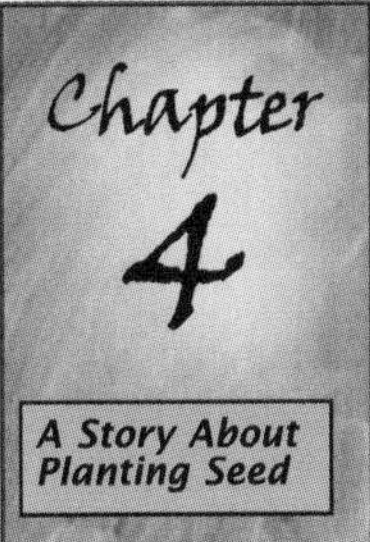
Chapter
4
A Story About
Planting Seed

1 Another time Jesus
began teaching by
the lake. A great
crowd gathered
around him. So he
got into a boat and
went out on the lake.
All the people stayed
on the shore close to
the water. 2 Jesus
used many stories to
teach them. He said,

3 "Listen! A farmer went
out to plant his seed. 4 While

the farmer was planting,
some seed fell by the
road. The birds came and
ate all that seed.

5 Some seed fell on rocky
ground where there wasn't
much dirt. The seed grew
very fast there because the
ground was not deep. 6 But
when the sun rose, the plants

withered. The plants died
because they did not have
deep roots.

7 Some other seed fell
among thorny weeds. The
weeds grew and choked the
good plants. So those plants
did not make grain.

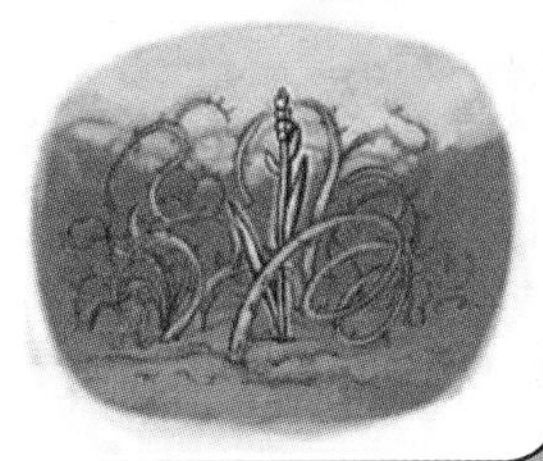

8 "Some other seed fell on good
ground. In the good ground, the seed
began to grow. It grew and made a crop
of grain. Some plants made 30 times
more grain, some 60 times more grain,
and some 100 times more grain."

9 Then Jesus said,

"Let those with ears
use them and listen!"

Jesus Tells Why He Used Stories

10 Later, when Jesus
was alone, the 12
apostles[d] and others
around him asked
him about the stories.
11 Jesus said,

"Only you can know the
secret truth about the kingdom of God. But to other
people I tell everything by
using stories. 12 I do this
so that:

> 'They will look and look,
> but they will not learn.
> They will listen and
> listen, but they will not
> understand. If they did
> learn and understand,
> they would come back
> to me and be forgiven.' "
>
> *Isaiah 6:9-10*

Jesus Explains the Seed Story

13 Then Jesus said to
the followers,

"Do you understand this
story? If you don't, then
how will you understand
any story? 14 The farmer is
like a person who plants
God's teaching in people.
15 Sometimes the teaching
falls on the road. This is

like some people. They
hear the teaching of God.
But Satan quickly comes
and takes away the teach-
ing that was planted in

them. 16 Others are like
the seed planted on rocky
ground. They hear the
teaching and quickly accept

it with joy. 17 But they
don't allow the teaching to
go deep into their lives.
They keep it only a short
time. When trouble or per-
secution comes because of
the teaching, they quickly
give up. 18 Others are like
the seed planted among the
thorny weeds. They hear
the teaching. 19 But then
other things come into
their lives: worries, the love
of money, and wanting all
kinds of other things.
These things stop the
teaching from growing. So
that teaching does not produce fruit[n] in their lives.

4:19 produce fruit To produce fruit means to have in your life the good things God wants.

20 "Others are like the
seed planted in the good
ground. They hear the teaching and accept it. Then they
grow and produce fruit—
sometimes 30 times more,
sometimes 60 times more,
and sometimes 100 times
more."

Use What You Have

21 Then Jesus said to them,

"Do you hide a lamp under a
bowl or under a bed? No! You
put the lamp on a lampstand.
22 Everything that is hidden
will be made clear. Every
secret thing will be made
known. 23 Let those with ears
use them and listen!
24 "Think carefully about the
things you hear. The way you
give to others is the way
God will give to you. But God
will give you more than you
give. 25 The person who has
something will be given more.
But the person who does not
have much, even what he has
will be taken from him."

Jesus Uses a Story About Seed

26 Then Jesus said,

"The kingdom of God is like a
man who plants seed in the
ground. 27 The seed comes
up and grows night and day.
It doesn't matter whether the
man is asleep or awake; the
seed still grows. The man
does not know how it grows.
28 Without any help, the earth
produces grain. First the plant
grows, then the head, and
then all the grain in the head.
29 When the grain is ready,
the man cuts it. This is the
harvest time."

A Story About Mustard Seed

30 Then Jesus said,

"How can I show you what the
kingdom of God is like? What
story can I use to explain it?
31 The kingdom of God is like
a mustard seed. The mustard
seed is the smallest seed you
plant in the ground. 32 But
when you plant this seed, it
grows and becomes the
largest of all garden plants. It
produces large branches.
Even the wild birds can make
nests in it and be protected
from the sun."

33 Jesus used many stories
like these to teach them. He
taught them all that they
could understand. 34 He
always used stories to teach
them. But when he and his
followers were alone
together, Jesus explained
everything to them.

Jesus Stops a Storm
35 That evening, Jesus said to his followers,
"Come with me across the lake."
36 He and the followers left the people there. They went in the boat that Jesus was already sitting in. There were also other boats with them. 37 A very strong wind came up on the lake. The waves began coming over the sides and into the boat. It was almost full of water.
38 Jesus was at the back of the boat, sleeping with his head on a pillow. The followers went to him and woke him. They said,
"Teacher, do you care about us? We will drown!"
39 Jesus stood up
and commanded the wind and the waves to stop. He said,
"Quiet! Be still!"

Then the wind stopped, and the lake became calm.

40 Jesus said to his followers,

"Why are you afraid? Do you still have no faith?"

41 The followers were very afraid and asked each other,

"What kind of man is this? Even the wind and the waves obey him!"

Chapter 5

A Man with Demons Inside Him

1 Jesus and his followers went across the lake to the region of the Gerasene[n] people. 2 When Jesus got out of the boat, a man came to him from the caves where dead people were buried. This man, who lived in the caves, had an evil spirit living in him. 3 No one could tie him up, not even with a chain.

4 Many times people had used chains to tie the man's hands and feet. But he always broke the chains off. No one was strong enough to control him. 5 Day and night he would wander around the burial caves and on the hills, screaming and cutting himself with stones. 6 While Jesus was still far away, the man saw him.

He ran to Jesus and knelt down before him. 7-8 Jesus said to the man,

"You evil spirit, come out of that man."

But the man shouted in a loud voice,

"What do you want with me, Jesus, Son of the Most High God? I beg you, promise God that you will not punish me!"

9 Then Jesus asked the man,

"What is your name?"

The man answered,

"My name is Legion,[n] because I have many spirits in me."

10 The man begged Jesus again and again not to send the spirits out of that area.

11 A large herd of pigs was eating on a hill near there.

5:1 Gerasene From Gerasa, an area southeast of Lake Galilee. The exact location is uncertain and some Greek copies read, "Gergesene"; others read "Gadarene."

5:9 Legion Means very many. A legion was about 5,000 men in the Roman army.

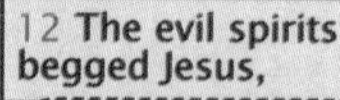

12 The evil spirits begged Jesus,

"Send us to the pigs. Let us go into them."

13 So Jesus allowed them to do this. The evil spirits left the man and went into the pigs. Then the herd of pigs rushed down the hill into the lake and were drowned. There were about 2,000 pigs in that herd.

14 The men who took care of the pigs ran away. They went to the town and to the countryside, telling everyone about this. So people went out to see what had happened. 15 They came to Jesus and saw the man who had had the many evil spirits. The man was sitting there, clothed and in his right mind. The people were frightened.

16 Some people were there who saw what Jesus had done. They told the others what had happened to the man who had the demons[d] living in him. And they also told about the pigs. 17 Then the people began to beg Jesus to leave their area.

18 Jesus was getting ready to leave in the boat. The man who was freed from the demons begged to go with him.

19 But Jesus would not allow the man to go. Jesus said,

"Go home to your family and friends. Tell them how much the Lord has done for you and how he has had mercy on you."

20 So the man left and told the people in the Ten Towns[n] about the great things Jesus had done for him. All the people were amazed.

Jesus Gives Life to a Dead Girl and Heals a Sick Woman

21 Jesus went in the boat back to the other side of the lake. There, a large crowd gathered around him.

5:20 Ten Towns In Greek, called "Decapolis." It was an area east of Lake Galilee that once had ten main towns.

22 A ruler from the synagogue,[d] named Jairus, came to that place. Jairus saw Jesus and bowed before him. 23 The ruler begged Jesus again and again. He said,

"My little daughter is dying. Please come and put your hands on her. Then she will be healed and will live."

24 So Jesus went with the ruler, and many people followed Jesus. They were pushing very close around him. 25 A woman was there who had been bleeding for the past 12 years. 26 She had suffered very much.

Many doctors had tried to help her. She had spent all the money she had, but she was not improving. She was getting worse. 27 When the woman heard about Jesus, she followed him with the people and touched his coat. 28 The woman thought,

"If I can even touch his coat, that will be enough to heal me."

29 When she touched his coat, her bleeding stopped. She could feel in her body that she was healed. 30 At once Jesus felt power go out from him. So he stopped and turned around.

Then he asked,
"Who touched my clothes?"
31 The followers said,
"There are so many people pushing against you! And you ask, 'Who touched me?' "
32 But Jesus continued looking around to see who had touched him. 33 The woman knew that she was healed. So she came and bowed at Jesus' feet. Shaking with fear, she told him the whole story. 34 Jesus said to the woman,

"Dear woman, you are made well because you believed. Go in peace. You will have no more suffering."
35 Jesus was still speaking to her when some men came from the house of Jairus, the synagogue ruler. The men said,
"Your daughter is dead. There is now no need to bother the teacher."

36 But Jesus paid no attention to what the men said. He said to the synagogue ruler,
"Don't be afraid; only believe."
37 Jesus let only Peter, James, and John the brother of James go with him to Jairus's house. 38 They came to the house of the synagogue ruler, and Jesus found many people there crying loudly. There was much confusion.

39 Jesus entered the house and said to the people,
"Why are you crying and making so much noise? This child is not dead. She is only asleep."
40 But they only laughed at Jesus.

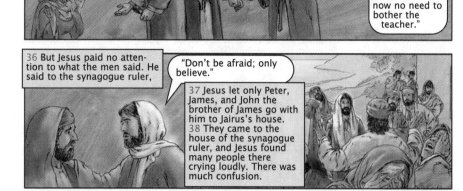

He told all the people to leave. Then he went into the room where the child was. He took the child's father and mother and his three followers into the room with him.

41 Then
he took
hold of
the girl's
hand and
said to
her,

"Talitha, koum!"

(This means, "Little girl, I tell you to stand up!")

42 The girl stood
right up and began
walking. (She was 12
years old.) The father
and mother and the
followers were
amazed. 43 Jesus
gave the father and
mother strict orders
not to tell people
about this. Then he
told them to give the
girl some food.

Chapter
6
Jesus Goes to His Hometown

1 Jesus left there and went
back to his hometown. His
followers went with him.
2 On the Sabbath[d] day he
taught in the synagogue.[d]
Many people heard him and
were amazed. They said,

"Where did this man get these teachings? What is this wisdom that has been given to him? And where did he get the power to work miracles?[d]

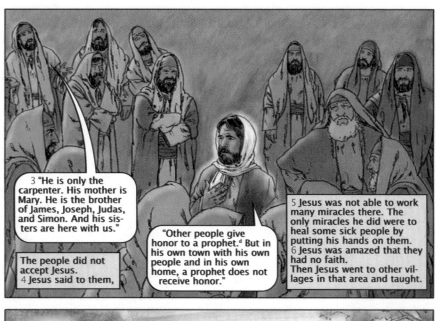

3 "He is only the carpenter. His mother is Mary. He is the brother of James, Joseph, Judas, and Simon. And his sisters are here with us."

The people did not accept Jesus.
4 Jesus said to them,

"Other people give honor to a prophet.[d] But in his own town with his own people and in his own home, a prophet does not receive honor."

5 Jesus was not able to work many miracles there. The only miracles he did were to heal some sick people by putting his hands on them.
6 Jesus was amazed that they had no faith.
Then Jesus went to other villages in that area and taught.

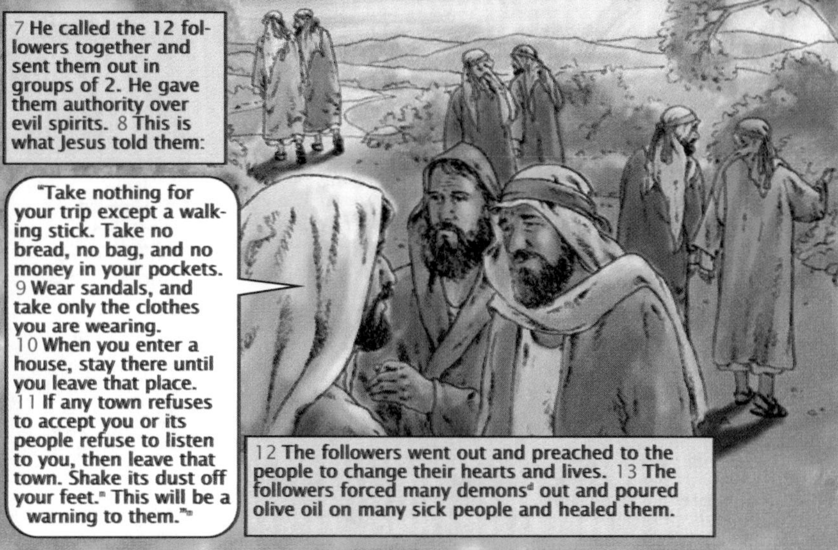
7 He called the 12 followers together and sent them out in groups of 2. He gave them authority over evil spirits. 8 This is what Jesus told them:
"Take nothing for your trip except a walking stick. Take no bread, no bag, and no money in your pockets.
9 Wear sandals, and take only the clothes you are wearing.
10 When you enter a house, stay there until you leave that place.
11 If any town refuses to accept you or its people refuse to listen to you, then leave that town. Shake its dust off your feet.[n] This will be a warning to them."[n]
12 The followers went out and preached to the people to change their hearts and lives. 13 The followers forced many demons[d] out and poured olive oil on many sick people and healed them.

6:11 Shake . . . feet. A warning. It showed that they were finished talking to these people.
6:11 them Some Greek copies continue, "I tell you the truth, on the Judgment Day it will be better for the towns of Sodom and Gomorrah than for the people of that town." See Matthew 10:15.

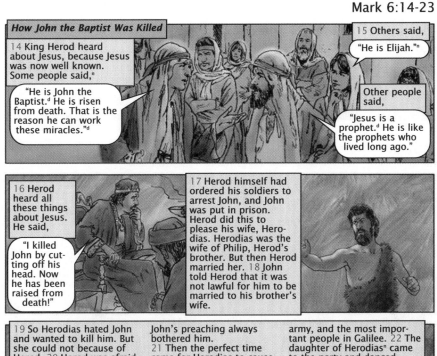

How John the Baptist Was Killed
14 King Herod heard about Jesus, because Jesus was now well known. Some people said,[n]
"He is John the Baptist.[d] He is risen from death. That is the reason he can work these miracles."[d]
15 Others said,
"He is Elijah."[n]
Other people said,
"Jesus is a prophet.[d] He is like the prophets who lived long ago."

16 Herod
heard all
these things
about Jesus.
He said,

"I killed
John by cut-
ting off his
head. Now
he has been
raised from
death!"

17 Herod himself had
ordered his soldiers to
arrest John, and John
was put in prison.
Herod did this to
please his wife, Hero-
dias. Herodias was the
wife of Philip, Herod's
brother. But then Herod
married her. 18 John
told Herod that it was
not lawful for him to be
married to his brother's
wife.

19 So Herodias hated John
and wanted to kill him. But
she could not because of
Herod. 20 Herod was afraid
to kill John because he knew
John was a good and holy
man. So Herod protected
John. Also, Herod enjoyed lis-
tening to John preach. But
John's preaching always
bothered him.
21 Then the perfect time
came for Herodias to cause
John's death. It happened on
Herod's birthday. Herod gave
a dinner party for the most
important government leaders, the commanders of his
army, and the most impor-
tant people in Galilee. 22 The
daughter of Herodias[n] came
to the party and danced.
When she danced, Herod and
the people eating with him
were very pleased.
So King Herod said to the
girl,

"I will give you anything you want."
23 He promised her,
"Anything you ask for I will give to you. I will even give you half of my kingdom."

6:14 Some people said Some Greek copies read "He said."
6:15 Elijah A man who spoke for God. He lived hundreds of years before Christ.
6:22 The . . . Herodias Some Greek copies read "His daughter Herodias."

24 The girl went to her mother and asked,

"What should I ask the king to give me?"

Her mother answered,

"Ask for the head of John the Baptist."[d]

25 Quickly the girl went back to the king. She said to him,

"Please give me the head of John the Baptist. Bring it to me now on a platter."

26 The king was very sad. But he had promised to give the girl anything she wanted. And the people eating there with him had heard his promise. So Herod could not refuse what she asked.

27 Immediately the king sent a soldier to bring John's head. The soldier went and cut off John's head in the prison 28 and brought it back on a platter. He gave it to the girl, and the girl gave it to her mother.

29 John's followers heard about what happened. So they came and got John's body and put it in a tomb.

More than 5,000 People Fed

30 The apostles[d] that Jesus had sent out to preach returned. They gathered around him and told him about all the things they had done and taught. 31 Crowds of people were coming and going. Jesus and his followers did not even have time to eat. He said to them,

"Come with me. We will go to a quiet place to be alone. There we will get some rest."

32 So they went in a boat alone to a place where there were no people. 33 But many people saw them leave and recognized them. So people from all the towns ran to the place where Jesus was going. They got there before Jesus arrived.

34 When he landed,
he saw a great crowd
waiting. Jesus felt
sorry for them,
because they were like
sheep without a shep-
herd. So he taught
them many things.
35 It was now late in
the day. Jesus' follow-
ers came to him and
said,

"No one lives
in this place. And it
is already very late.
36 Send the people
away. They need to
go to the farms and
towns around here
to buy some food
to eat."

37 But Jesus
answered,

"You give them
food to eat."

They said to him,

"We can't buy enough bread to feed all these
people! We would all have to work a month to
earn enough money to buy that much bread!"

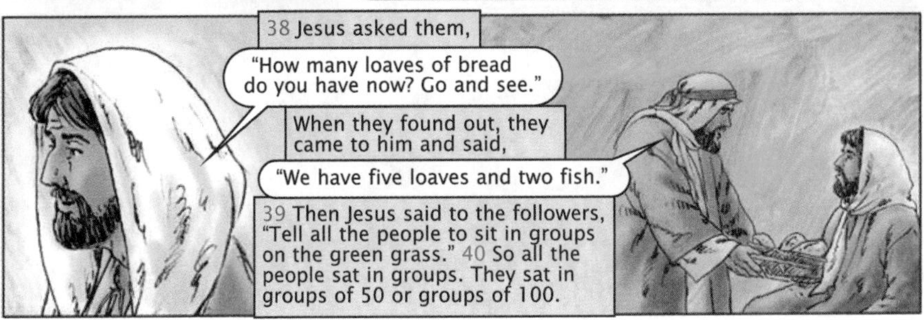
38 Jesus asked them,
"How many loaves of bread
do you have now? Go and see."
When they found out, they
came to him and said,
"We have five loaves and two fish."
39 Then Jesus said to the followers,
"Tell all the people to sit in groups
on the green grass." 40 So all the
people sat in groups. They sat in
groups of 50 or groups of 100.

41 Jesus took the five loaves
and two fish. He looked up to
heaven and thanked God for
the bread. He divided the
bread and gave it to his
followers for them to give to
the people. Then he divided
the two fish among them all.

42 All the people ate and were satisfied.
43 The followers filled 12 baskets with the
pieces of bread and fish that were not eaten.
44 There were about 5,000 men there who ate.

Jesus Walks on the Water

45 Then Jesus told
his followers to get
into the boat and
go to Bethsaida on
the other side of
the lake. Jesus said
that he would
come later. He
stayed there to tell
the people they
could go home.

46 After
sending them
away, he
went into the
hills to pray.

47 That night, the boat
was in the middle of the
lake. Jesus was alone on
the land. 48 He saw the
followers working hard to
row the boat because the
wind was blowing against
them. At some time
between three and six
o'clock in the morning,
Jesus came to them, walk-
ing on the water. He con-
tinued walking until he
was almost past the boat.

49 But when his
followers saw him
walking on the
water, they thought
he was a ghost and
cried out. 50 They
all saw him and
were terrified. But
Jesus spoke to
them and said,

"Have courage! It is
I! Do not be afraid."

51 Then he got into the boat
with them. And the wind
became calm. The followers
were greatly amazed. 52 They
had seen Jesus make more
bread from the five loaves. But
they did not understand what it
meant. Their minds were closed.

53 When they had
crossed the lake, they
came to shore at
Gennesaret. They tied
the boat there. 54 When
they got out of the boat,
the people saw Jesus
and immediately recog-
nized him. 55 They ran
to tell others everywhere
in that area that Jesus
was there. They brought
sick people on mats to
every place Jesus went.

56 Jesus went into
towns and cities and
farms around that
area. And everywhere
he went, the people
brought the sick to
the marketplaces.
They begged him to
let them just touch
the edge of his coat.
And all who touched
him were healed.

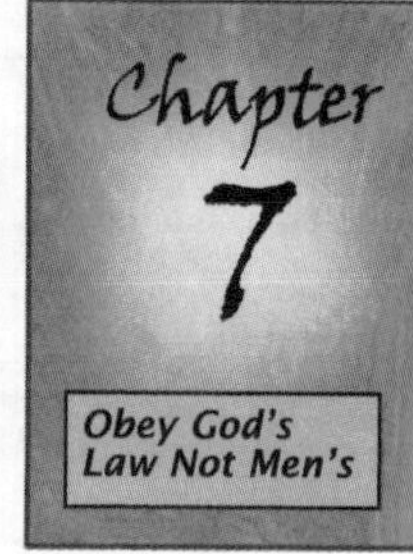
Chapter
7
Obey God's Law Not Men's

1 Some Pharisees[d] and some
teachers of the law came
from Jerusalem. They gathered around Jesus. 2 They
saw that some of Jesus' followers ate food with hands
that were not clean.[d] ("Not
clean" means that they did
not wash their hands in the
way the Pharisees said people
must. 3 The Pharisees and all
the Jews never eat before
washing their hands in this
special way. They do this to
follow the teaching given to
them by their great people
who lived before them.

4 And when the Jews buy something in the market, they never
eat it until they wash it in a
special way. They also follow
other rules of their great people
who lived before them. They
follow rules about the washing
of cups, pitchers, and pots.[n])
5 The Pharisees and the teachers of the law said to Jesus,

"Your followers don't follow the rules given to us by our great people who lived before us. Your followers eat their food with hands that are not clean. Why do they do this?"

6 Jesus answered,

"You are all hypocrites![d] Isaiah was right when he spoke about you. Isaiah wrote,

'These people show
honor to me with words.
But their hearts are far
from me. 7 Their worship
of me is worthless. The
things they teach are
nothing but human rules
they have memorized.'
Isaiah 29:13

8 You have stopped following the commands of God.
Now you only follow the
teachings of men."[n]

7:4 pots Some Greek copies continue, "and dining couches." **7:8 teachings of men** Some Greek copies continue, "You wash pitchers and jugs and do many other such things."

9 Then Jesus said to them:
"You think you are clever! You ignore the commands of God so that you can follow your own teachings! 10 Moses said, 'Honor your father and mother.'[n] Then Moses also said, 'Anyone who says cruel things to his father or mother must be put to death.'[n] 11 But you teach that a person can say to his father or mother, 'I have something I could use to help you. But I will not use it for you. I will give it to God.' 12 You are telling that person that he does not have to do anything for his father or mother. 13 So you are teaching that it is not important to do what God said. You think that it is more important to follow your own rules, which you teach people. And you do many things like that."

14 Jesus called the people to him again. He said,
"Every person should listen to me and understand what I am saying. 15 There is nothing a person puts into his body that makes him unclean. A person is made unclean by the things that come out of him." 16 [Let those with ears use them and listen.]"[n]

17 When Jesus left the people and went inside, his followers asked him about this story. 18 Jesus said,
"Do you still have trouble understanding? Surely you know that nothing that enters a man from the outside can make him unclean.

7:10 'Honor . . . mother.' Quotation from Exodus 20:12; Deuteronomy 5:16.
7:10 'Anyone . . . death.' Quotation from Exodus 21:17.
7:16 Let . . . listen. Some Greek copies do not contain the bracketed text.

19 "Food does not go into a person's mind. Food goes into his stomach. Then that food goes out of his body."

(When Jesus said this, he meant that there is no food that is unclean for people to eat.)
20 And Jesus said,

"The things that come out of a man are the things that make him unclean. 21 All these evil things begin inside a person, in his mind: evil thoughts, sexual sins, stealing, murder, adultery,[d] 22 selfishness, doing bad things to other people, lying, doing sinful things, jealousy, saying bad things about people, pride, and foolish living. 23 All these evil things come from within a person. These things make a person unclean."

Jesus Helps a Non-Jewish Woman

24 Jesus left that place and went to the area around Tyre.[n] He went into a house and did not want anyone to know he was there. But Jesus could not stay hidden. 25 A woman heard that he was there. Her little daughter had an evil spirit in her. So the woman quickly came to Jesus and fell at his feet.

26 She was not Jewish. She was Greek, born in Phoenicia, in Syria. She begged Jesus to force the demon[d] out of her daughter.
27 Jesus told the woman:

"It is not right to take the children's bread and give it to the dogs. First let the children eat all they want."

28 She answered,

"That is true, Lord. But the dogs under the table can eat the pieces of food that the children don't eat."

7:24 Tyre Some Greek copies continue, "and Sidon."

29 Then Jesus said,

"That is a very good answer. You may go. The demon has left your daughter."

30 The woman went home and found her daughter lying in bed. The demon was gone.

Jesus Heals a Deaf Man

31 Then Jesus left the area around Tyre. He went through Sidon to Lake Galilee, to the area of the Ten Towns.[a]

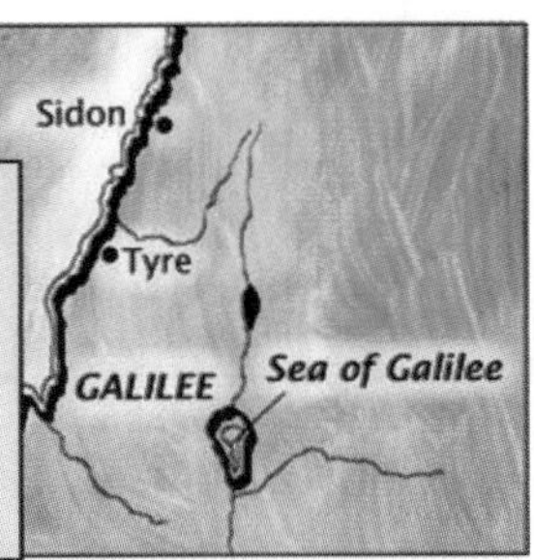
Sidon
Tyre
GALILEE
Sea of Galilee

32 While he was there, some people brought a man to him. This man was deaf and could not talk. The people begged Jesus to put his hand on the man to heal him. 33 Jesus led the man away from the crowd, to be alone with him. Jesus put his fingers in the man's ears.

Then Jesus spit and touched the man's tongue.

34 Jesus looked up to heaven and took a deep breath. He said to the man,

"Ephphatha!"

(This means, "Be opened.") 35 When Jesus did this, the man was able to hear. He was also able to use his tongue, and he spoke clearly.

36 Jesus commanded the people not to tell anyone about what happened. But the more he commanded them, the more they told about it. 37 They were really amazed. They said,

"Jesus does everything well. He makes the deaf hear! And those who can't talk—Jesus makes them able to speak."

7:31 Ten Towns In Greek, called "Decapolis." It was an area east of Lake Galilee that once had ten main towns.

Mark 8:1-9

Chapter 8

More than 4,000 People Fed

1 Another
time there
was a great
crowd with
Jesus. They
had nothing
to eat. So
Jesus called
his followers
to him. He
said,

2 "I feel sorry
for these people.
They have been with
me for three days,
and now they have
nothing to eat. 3 I
cannot send them
home hungry. If they
leave without eating,
they will faint on the
way home. Some of
them live a long way
from here."

4 Jesus' followers
answered,

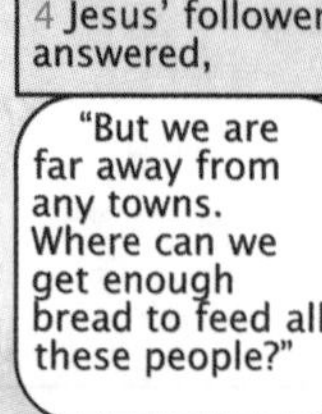

"But we are
far away from
any towns.
Where can we
get enough
bread to feed all
these people?"

5 Jesus asked,

"How many loaves of
bread do you have?"

They answered,

"We have seven loaves."

6 Jesus told the people
to sit on the ground.
Then he took the
seven loaves and gave
thanks to God. Jesus
divided the bread and
gave the pieces to his
followers. He told them
to pass out the bread
to the people, and they
did so. 7 The followers
also had a few small
fish. Jesus gave thanks
for the fish and told
his followers to give
the fish to the people.
8 All the people ate
and were satisfied.
Then the followers
filled seven baskets
with the pieces of food
that were not eaten.
9 There were about
4,000 men who ate.
After they had eaten,
Jesus told them to go
home.

10 Then he went in a boat with his followers to the area of Dalmanutha.

The Leaders Ask for a Miracle

11 The Pharisees[d] came to Jesus and asked him questions. They wanted to trap him. So they asked Jesus to do a miracle[d] to show that he was from God.
12 Jesus sighed deeply. He said,

"Why do you people ask for a miracle as proof? I tell you the truth. No miracle will be given to you."

13 Then Jesus left the Pharisees. He went in the boat to the other side of the lake.

Guard Against Wrong Teachings

14 The followers had only one loaf of bread with them in the boat. They had forgotten to bring more bread.
15 Jesus warned them,

"Be careful! Guard against the yeast of the Pharisees[d] and the yeast of Herod."

16 Among themselves, his disciples discussed the meaning of this. They said, "He said this because we have no bread."
17 Jesus knew what his followers were talking about. So he asked them,

"Why are you talking about having no bread? You still don't see or understand? Are your minds closed? 18 You have eyes, but you don't really see. You have ears, but you don't really listen.

Remember what I did before, when we did not have enough bread?
19 I divided five loaves of bread for 5,000 people. Remember how many baskets you filled with pieces of food that were not eaten?"

They answered,

"We filled 12 baskets."

20 "And remember that I divided seven loaves of bread for 4,000 people. Remember how many baskets you filled with pieces of food that were not eaten?"

They answered,

"We filled 7 baskets."

21 Then Jesus said to them,

"You remember these things I did, but you still don't understand?"

Jesus Heals a Blind Man

22 Jesus and his follow-
ers came to Bethsaida.
Some people brought a
blind man to Jesus and
begged him to touch
the man. 23 So Jesus
took the blind man's
hand and led him out of
the village. Then he spit
on the man's eyes. He
put his hands on the
blind man and asked,

"Can you see now?"

24 The man looked up and said,

"Yes, I see people, but they look like trees walking around."

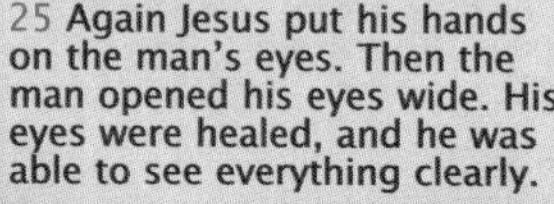
25 Again Jesus put his hands
on the man's eyes. Then the
man opened his eyes wide. His
eyes were healed, and he was
able to see everything clearly.

26 Jesus told him to
go home, saying,

"Don't go into the town."[n]

Peter Says Jesus Is the Christ

27 Jesus and his follow-
ers went to the towns
around Caesarea Philippi.
While they were travel-
ing, Jesus asked them,

"Who do people say I am?"

28 They answered,

"Some people say you are John the Baptist.[d] Others say you are Elijah.[n] And others say that you are one of the prophets."[d]

29 Then
Jesus asked,
"Who do you say I am?"
Peter answered,
"You are the Christ."[d]

30 Jesus ordered his followers,

"Don't tell anyone who I am."

8:26 town Some Greek copies continue, "Don't even go and tell anyone in the town."
8:28 Elijah A man who spoke for God. He lived hundreds of years before Christ.

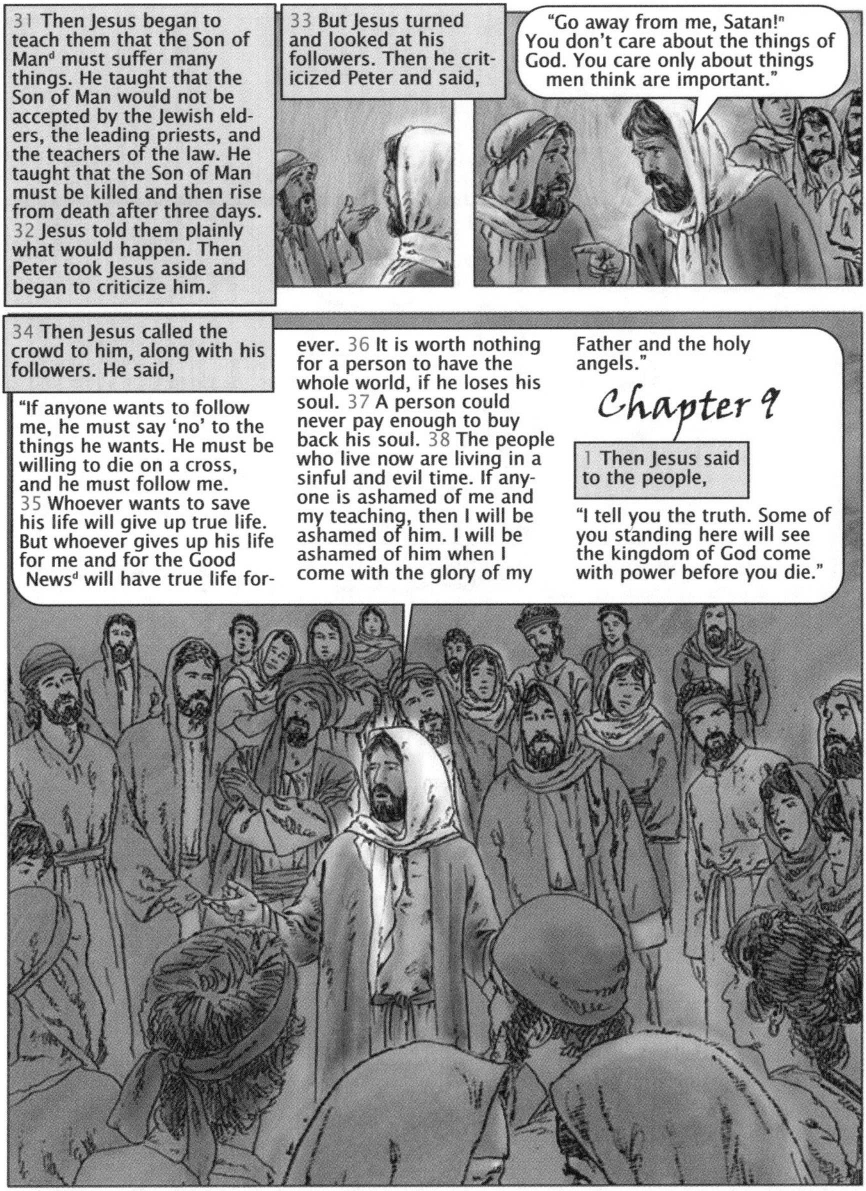

31 Then Jesus began to
teach them that the Son of
Man[d] must suffer many
things. He taught that the
Son of Man would not be
accepted by the Jewish elders, the leading priests, and
the teachers of the law. He
taught that the Son of Man
must be killed and then rise
from death after three days.
32 Jesus told them plainly
what would happen. Then
Peter took Jesus aside and
began to criticize him.

33 But Jesus turned
and looked at his
followers. Then he criticized Peter and said,

"Go away from me, Satan![n] You don't care about the things of God. You care only about things men think are important."

34 Then Jesus called the
crowd to him, along with his
followers. He said,

"If anyone wants to follow
me, he must say 'no' to the
things he wants. He must be
willing to die on a cross,
and he must follow me.
35 Whoever wants to save
his life will give up true life.
But whoever gives up his life
for me and for the Good
News[d] will have true life forever.
36 It is worth nothing
for a person to have the
whole world, if he loses his
soul.
37 A person could
never pay enough to buy
back his soul.
38 The people
who live now are living in a
sinful and evil time. If anyone is ashamed of me and
my teaching, then I will be
ashamed of him. I will be
ashamed of him when I
come with the glory of my
Father and the holy
angels."

Chapter 9

1 Then Jesus said
to the people,

"I tell you the truth. Some of
you standing here will see
the kingdom of God come
with power before you die."

8:33 Satan Name for the devil meaning "the enemy." Jesus means that Peter was talking like Satan.

Jesus with Moses and Elijah

2 Six days later Jesus took
Peter, James, and John and
went up on a high mountain.
They were all alone there.

While these fol-
lowers watched,
Jesus was
changed. 3 His
clothes became
shining white,
whiter than any
person could
make them.
4 Then two men
appeared, talking
with Jesus. The
men were Moses
and Elijah.[n]

5 Peter said to Jesus,

"Teacher, it
is good that we
are here. We will
put three tents
here—one for
you, one for
Moses, and one
for Elijah."

6 Peter did not know what to
say, because he and the others
were so frightened.

7 Then a cloud came and
covered them. A voice came
from the cloud. The voice said,

"This is my
Son, and I love
him. Obey him!"

8 Then Peter, James, and
John looked around, but
they saw only Jesus
there alone with them.

9 As Jesus and his followers were
walking back down the mountain, he commanded them,

"Don't tell anyone about
the things you saw on the
mountain. Wait till the Son of
Man[d] rises from death. Then
you may tell."

10 So the followers obeyed
Jesus and said nothing about
what they had seen. But they
discussed what Jesus meant
about rising from death.

11 They
asked Jesus,

"Why
do the
teachers of
the law say
that Elijah
must come
first?"

12 Jesus answered,

"They are right to say that
Elijah must come first. Elijah
makes all things the way they
should be. But why does the
Scripture[d] say that the Son of Man
will suffer much and that people
will treat him as if he were nothing? 13 I tell you that Elijah has
already come. And people did to
him whatever they wanted to do.
The Scriptures said this would
happen to him."

9:4 Moses and Elijah Two of the most important Jewish leaders in the past.

Jesus Heals a Sick Boy

14 Then Jesus, Peter,
James, and John went
to the other followers.
They saw a great crowd
around them. The
teachers of the law
were arguing with
them. 15 But when the
crowd saw Jesus, they
were surprised and ran
to welcome him.
16 Jesus asked,

"What are you arguing about with the teachers of the law?"
17 A man answered,
"Teacher, I brought my son to you. He has a spirit from the devil in him. This spirit stops him from talking.

18 The spirit attacks him and throws him on the ground. My son foams at the mouth, grinds his teeth, and becomes very stiff. I asked your followers to force the evil spirit out, but they couldn't."

19 Jesus answered,
"You people don't believe! How long must I stay with you? How long must I go on being patient with you? Bring the boy to me!"

20 So the followers brought
him to Jesus. As soon as the
evil spirit saw Jesus, it
attacked the boy. He fell down
and rolled on the ground,
foaming from his mouth.

21 Jesus asked the
boy's father,

"How long has this been happening?"

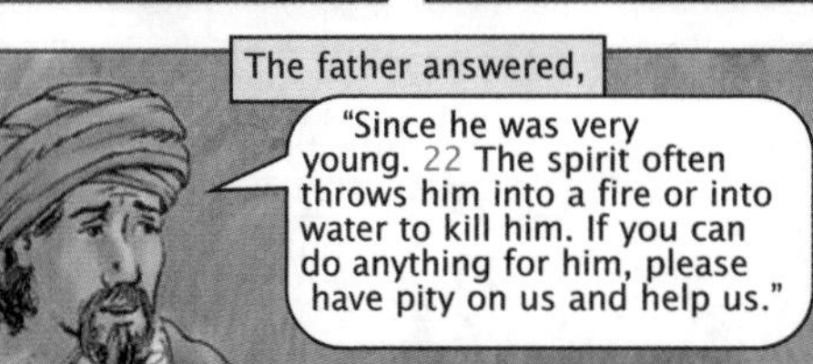

The father answered,
"Since he was very young. 22 The spirit often throws him into a fire or into water to kill him. If you can do anything for him, please have pity on us and help us."
23 Jesus said to the father,
"You said, 'If you can!' All things are possible for him who believes."

24 Immediately the father cried out,
"I do believe! Help me to believe more!"
25 Jesus saw that a crowd was running there to see what was happening. So he spoke to the evil spirit, saying,
"You deaf and dumb spirit—I command you to come out of this boy and never enter him again!"

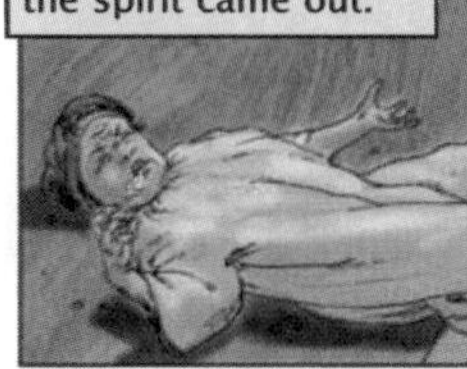
26 The evil spirit screamed and caused the boy to fall on the ground again. Then the spirit came out.

The boy looked as if he were dead. And many people said,

"He is dead!"

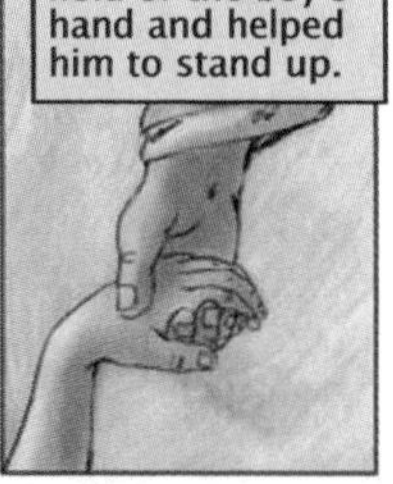
27 But Jesus took hold of the boy's hand and helped him to stand up.

28 Jesus went into the house. His followers were alone with him there. They said,

"Why couldn't we force that evil spirit out?"
29 Jesus answered,
"That kind of spirit can only be forced out by prayer."

Jesus Talks About His Death

30 Then Jesus and his followers left that place and went through Galilee. Jesus did not want anyone to know where he was 31 because he wanted to teach his followers alone. He said to them,

"The Son of Man[d] will be given to men who will kill him. After three days, he will rise from death."

32 But the followers did not understand what Jesus meant. And they were afraid to ask.

Who Is the Greatest?

33 Jesus and his followers went to Capernaum and went into a house there.

Then Jesus said to them,

"What were you arguing about on the road?"

34 But the followers did not answer, because their argument on the road was about which one of them was the greatest.

35 Jesus sat down and called the 12 apostles[d] to him. He said,

"If anyone wants to be the most important, then he must be last of all and servant of all."

36 Then Jesus took a small child and had him stand among them. He took the child in his arms and said,

37 "If anyone accepts children like these in my name, then he is also accepting me. And if he accepts me, then he is also accepting the One who sent me."

Anyone Not Against Us Is for Us

38 Then John said,

"Teacher, we saw a man using your name to force demons[d] out of a person. We told him to stop, because he does not belong to our group."

39 Jesus said,

"Don't stop him. Anyone who uses my name to do powerful things will not say evil things about me. 40 He who is not against us is with us. 41 I tell you the truth. If anyone helps you by giving you a drink of water because you belong to the Christ,[d] then he will truly get his reward.

42 "If one of these little children believes in me, and someone causes that child to sin, then it will be very bad for him. It would be better for him to have a large stone tied around his neck and be drowned in the sea.

43 If your hand causes you to sin, cut it off. It is better for you to lose part of your body but have life forever. That is much better than to have two hands and go to hell. In that place the fire never goes out. 44 [In hell the worm does not die; the fire is never stopped.][n]

9:44 In . . . stopped. Some Greek copies do not contain the bracketed text.

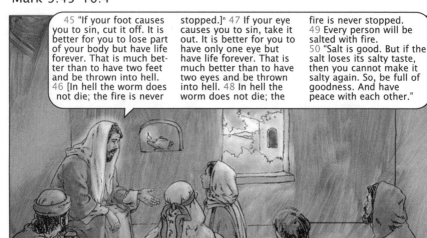

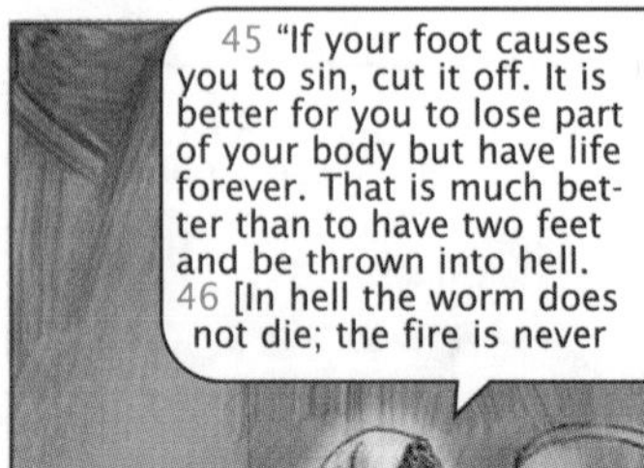

45 "If your foot causes you to sin, cut it off. It is better for you to lose part of your body but have life forever. That is much better than to have two feet and be thrown into hell.
46 [In hell the worm does not die; the fire is never stopped.][n] 47 If your eye causes you to sin, take it out. It is better for you to have only one eye but have life forever. That is much better than to have two eyes and be thrown into hell. 48 In hell the worm does not die; the fire is never stopped.
49 Every person will be salted with fire.
50 "Salt is good. But if the salt loses its salty taste, then you cannot make it salty again. So, be full of goodness. And have peace with each other."

Chapter 10
Jesus Teaches About Divorce

1 Then Jesus left that place. He went into the area of Judea and across the Jordan River. Again, crowds came to him. And Jesus taught them as he always did.

2 Some Pharisees[d] came to Jesus and tried to trick him. They asked,
"Is it right for a man to divorce his wife?"
3 Jesus answered,
"What did Moses command you to do?"
4 They said,
"Moses allowed a man to write out divorce papers and send her away."[n]

9:46 In . . . stopped. Some Greek copies do not contain the bracketed text.
10:4 "Moses . . . away." Quotation from Deuteronomy 24:1.

5 Jesus said,

"Moses wrote that command for
you because you refused to accept
God's teaching. 6 But when God
made the world, 'he made them male
and female.'[n] 7 'So a man will leave
his father and mother and be united
with his wife.[n] 8 And the two people
will become one body.'[n] So the people are not two, but one. 9 God has
joined the two people together. So
no one should separate them."

10 Later, the followers and
Jesus were in the house.
They asked Jesus again
about the question of
divorce. 11 He answered,

"Anyone who divorces
his wife and marries
another woman is guilty of
adultery[d] against her.
12 And the woman who di-
vorces her husband and
marries another man is
also guilty of adultery."

Jesus Accepts Children

13 Some people
brought their small
children to Jesus so he
could touch them. But
his followers told the
people to stop bringing
their children to him.
14 When Jesus saw
this, he was displeased.
He said to them,

"Let the little chil-
dren come to me. Don't
stop them. The kingdom
of God belongs to peo-
ple who are like these
little children. 15 I tell
you the truth. You must
accept the kingdom of
God as a little child
accepts things, or you
will never enter it."

16 Then Jesus took the
children in his arms. He
put his hands on them
and blessed them.

10:6 'he made . . . female.' Quotation from Genesis 1:27.
10:7 and . . . wife Some Greek copies do not have this phrase.
10:7-8 'So . . . body.' Quotation from Genesis 2:24.

A Rich Young Man's Question

17 Jesus started to leave, but a man ran to him and fell on his knees before Jesus. The man asked,
"Good teacher, what must I do to get the life that never ends?"
18 Jesus answered,
"Why do you call me good? No one is good except God alone. 19 You know the commands: 'You must not murder anyone. You must not be guilty of adultery.[d] You must not steal. You must not tell lies about your neighbor in court. You must not cheat. Honor your father and mother.' "[n]

20 The man said,
"Teacher, I have obeyed all these commands since I was a boy."

21 Jesus looked straight at the man and loved him. Jesus said,
"There is still one more thing you need to do. Go and sell everything you have, and give the money to the poor. You will have a reward in heaven. Then come and follow me."
22 He was very sad to hear Jesus say this, and he left. The man was sad because he was very rich.

23 Then Jesus looked at his followers and said,
"How hard it will be for those who are rich to enter the kingdom of God!"
24 The followers were amazed at what Jesus said. But he said again,
"My children, it is very hard[n] to enter the kingdom of God!

25 And it will be very hard for a rich person to enter the kingdom of God. It would be easier for a camel to go through the eye of a needle!"

26 The followers were even more amazed and said to each other,
"Then who can be saved?"

27 Jesus looked straight at them and said,
"For people this is impossible. But for God all things are possible."

10:19 'You . . . mother.' Quotation from Exodus 20:12-16; Deuteronomy 5:16-20.
10:24 hard Some Greek copies continue, "for those who trust in riches."

28 Peter said to Jesus,

"We left everything to follow you!"

29 Jesus said,

"I tell you the truth. Everyone who has left his home, brothers, sisters, mother, father, children, or fields for me and for the Good News[d] 30 will get a hundred times more than he left. Here in this world he will have more homes, brothers, sisters, mothers, children, and fields. And with those things, he will also suffer for his belief.

But in this age he will have life forever. 31 Many who are first now will be last in the future. And those who are last now will be first in the future."

Jesus Talks About His Own Death

32 Jesus and the people with him were on the road to Jerusalem. Jesus was leading the way. The followers were amazed, but those who followed behind them were afraid. Jesus took the 12 apostles[d] aside and talked with them alone. He told them what would happen in Jerusalem.

33 He said,

"We are going to Jerusalem. The Son of Man[d] will be given to the leading priests and teachers of the law. They will say that he must die. They will give him to the non-Jewish people, 34 who will laugh at him and spit on him. They will beat him with whips and kill him. But on the third day after his death, he will rise to life again."

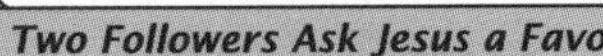

Two Followers Ask Jesus a Favor

35 Then James and John, sons of Zebedee, came to Jesus. They said,

"Teacher, we want to ask you to do something for us."

36 Jesus asked,

"What do you want me to do for you?"

37 They answered,

"You will have glory in your kingdom. Let one of us sit at your right, and let one of us sit at your left."

38 Jesus said,
"You don't understand what you are asking. Can you drink the cup that I must drink? And can you be baptized with the same kind of baptism that I must have?"[n]
39 They answered,
"Yes, we can!"
Jesus said to them,
"You will drink the same cup that I will drink. And you will be baptized with the same baptism that I must have.

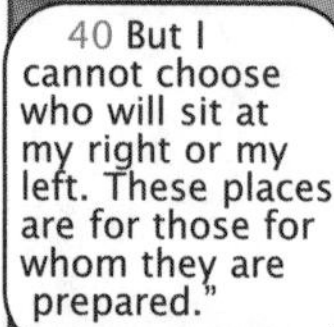
40 But I cannot choose who will sit at my right or my left. These places are for those for whom they are prepared."

41 The ten followers heard this. They began to be angry with James and John.
42 Jesus called all the followers together. He said,

"The non-Jewish people have men they call rulers. You know that those rulers love to show their power over the people. And their important leaders love to use all their authority. 43 But it should not be that way among you. If one of you wants to become great, then he must serve you like a servant. 44 If one of you wants to become the most important, then he must serve all of you like a slave. 45 In the same way, the Son of Man[d] did not come to be served. He came to serve. The Son of Man came to give his life to save many people."

Jesus Heals a Blind Man

46 Then they came to the town of Jericho. As Jesus was leaving there with his followers and a large crowd, a blind beggar named Bartimaeus (son of Timaeus) was sitting by the road.
47 He heard that Jesus from Nazareth was walking by. The blind man cried out,
"Jesus, Son of David,[d] please help me!"

48 Many people scolded the blind man and told him to be quiet. But he shouted more and more,

"Son of David, please help me!"

10:38 Can you . . . have? Jesus was asking if they could suffer the same terrible things that would happen to him.

49 Jesus stopped and said,
"Tell the man to come here."

So they called the blind man. They said,
"Cheer up! Get to your feet. Jesus is calling you."

50 The blind man stood up quickly. He left his coat there and went to Jesus.

51 Jesus asked him,
"What do you want me to do for you?"
The blind man answered,
"Teacher, I want to see again."

52 Jesus said,
"Go. You are healed because you believed."

At once the man was able to see again, and he followed Jesus on the road.

Chapter 11

Jesus Enters Jerusalem as a King

1 Jesus and his followers were coming closer to Jerusalem. They came to the towns of Bethphage and Bethany near the Mount of Olives.[d]

There Jesus sent two of his followers. 2 He said to them,
"Go to the town you see there. When you enter it, you will find a colt tied which no one has ever ridden. Untie it and bring it here to me. 3 If anyone asks you why you are doing this, tell him, 'The Master needs the colt. He will send it back soon.' "

4 The followers went into the town. They found a colt tied in the street near the door of a house, and they untied it.

5 Some people were standing there and asked,
"What are you doing? Why are you untying that colt?"
6 The followers answered the way Jesus told them to answer. And the people let them take the colt.
7 The followers brought the colt to Jesus. They put their coats on the colt, and Jesus sat on it.
8 Many people spread their coats on the road. Others cut branches in the fields and spread the branches on the road. 9 Some of the people were walking ahead of Jesus. Others were following him. All of them were shouting,
"Praise[n] God!
God bless the One who comes in the name of the Lord!
Psalm 118:26
10 God bless the kingdom of our father David! That kingdom is coming! Praise to God in heaven!"

11:9 Praise Literally, "Hosanna," a Hebrew word used at first in praying to God for help, but at this time it was probably a shout of joy used in praising God or his Messiah.

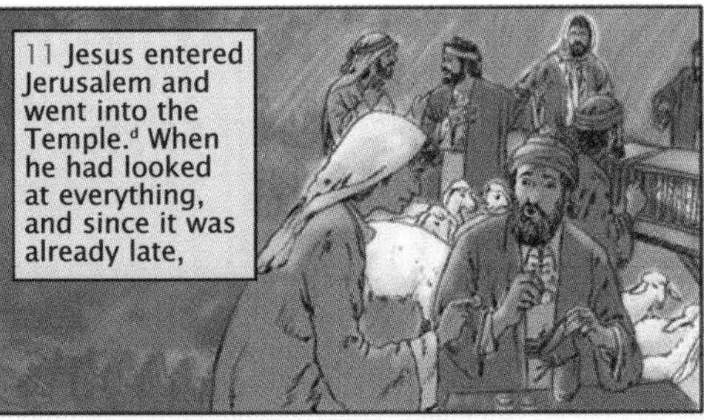
11 Jesus entered Jerusalem and went into the Temple.[d] When he had looked at everything, and since it was already late,

he went out to Bethany with the 12 apostles.[d]

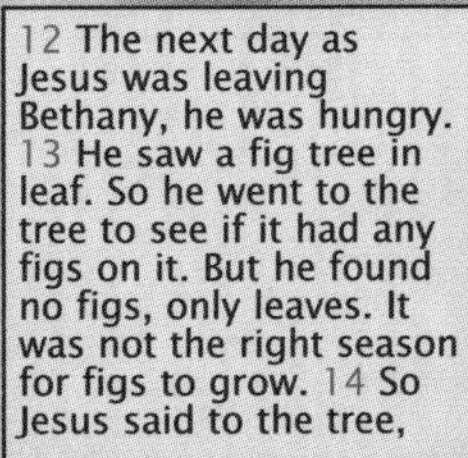
12 The next day as Jesus was leaving Bethany, he was hungry. 13 He saw a fig tree in leaf. So he went to the tree to see if it had any figs on it. But he found no figs, only leaves. It was not the right season for figs to grow. 14 So Jesus said to the tree,

"May no one ever eat fruit from you again."
Jesus' followers heard him say this.

Jesus Goes to the Temple

15 Jesus returned to
Jerusalem and went
into the Temple.[d] He
began to throw out
those who were buy-
ing and selling
things there. He
overturned the
tables that belonged
to the men who were
exchanging different
kinds of money. And
he turned over the
benches of the men
who were selling
doves. 16 Jesus
refused to allow any-
one to carry goods
through the Temple
courts. 17 Then
Jesus taught the
people. He said,

"It is written in the Scriptures,[d] 'My Temple will be a house where people from all nations will pray.'[n] But you are changing God's house into a 'hideout for robbers.' "[n]

11:17 'My Temple . . . pray.' Quotation from Isaiah 56:7.
11:17 'hideout for robbers.' Quotation from Jeremiah 7:11.

18 The leading priests and the teachers of the law heard all this. They began trying to find a way to kill Jesus. They were afraid of him because all the people were amazed at his teaching.

19 That night, Jesus and his followers[n] left the city.

The Power of Faith

20 The next morning, Jesus was passing by with his followers. They saw the fig tree, and it was dry and dead, even to the roots.

21 Peter remembered the tree and said to Jesus,

"Teacher, look! Yesterday, you cursed the fig tree. Now it is dry and dead!"

22 Jesus answered,

"Have faith in God.
23 I tell you the truth. You can say to this mountain, 'Go, mountain, fall into the sea.' And if you have no doubts in your mind and believe that the thing you say will happen, then God will do it for you.

24 So I tell you to ask for things in prayer. And if you believe that you have received those things, then they will be yours.
25 When you are praying, and you remember that you are angry with another person about something, then forgive him. If you do this, then your Father in heaven will also forgive your sins."

26 [But if you don't forgive other people, then your Father in heaven will not forgive your sins.][n]

Leaders Doubt Jesus' Authority

27 Jesus and his followers went again to Jerusalem. Jesus was walking in the Temple.[d] The leading priests, the teachers of the law, and the older Jewish leaders came to him.

11:19 his followers Some Greek copies mention only Jesus here.
11:26 But . . . sins. Some Greek copies do not contain the bracketed text.

28 They said to him,
"Tell us! What authority do you have to do these things? Who gave you this authority?"
29 Jesus answered,
"I will ask you one question. You answer it. Then I will tell you whose authority I use to do these things. 30 Tell me: When John baptized people, was that from God or from man? Answer me!"

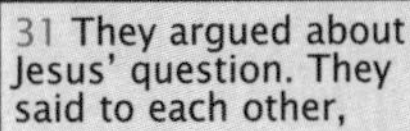
31 They argued about Jesus' question. They said to each other,

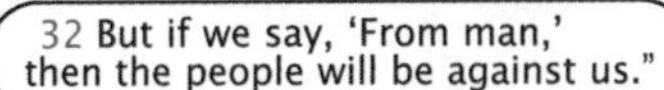
"If we answer, 'John's baptism was from God,' then Jesus will say, 'Then why didn't you believe John?'
32 But if we say, 'From man,' then the people will be against us."

(These leaders were afraid of the people. All the people believed that John was a prophet.[d])

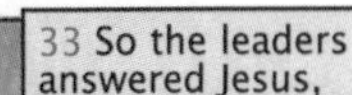
33 So the leaders answered Jesus,

"We don't know."

Jesus said,
"Then I will not tell you what authority I use to do these things."

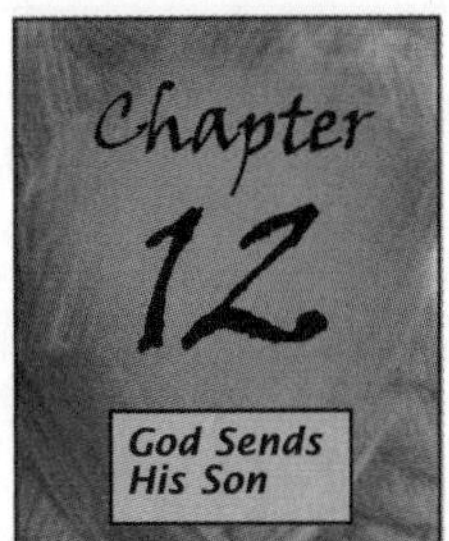
Chapter
12
God Sends His Son

1 Jesus used stories to teach the people. He said,
"A man planted a vineyard.

He put a wall around it and dug a hole for a winepress.[d] Then he built a tower.
He leased the vineyard to some farmers and left for a trip. 2 Later, it was time for

the grapes to be picked. So the man sent a servant to the farmers to get his share of the grapes.

3 "But the farmers grabbed
the servant and beat him.
They sent him away with

nothing. 4 Then the man sent
another servant. They hit him
on the head and showed no

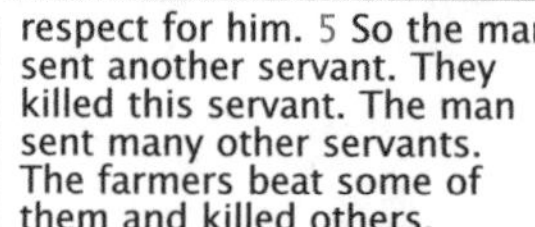

respect for him. 5 So the man
sent another servant. They
killed this servant. The man
sent many other servants.
The farmers beat some of
them and killed others.

6 "The man had one person
left to send, his son whom he
loved. He sent him last of all,
saying,

'The farmers will
respect my son.'

7 "But they said to each
other,

'This is the owner's
son. This vineyard will be
his. If we kill him, then it
will be ours.'

8 So they took the son, killed
him, and threw him out of
the vineyard.

9 "So what
will the man who
owns the vineyard
do? He will go to
the vineyard and
kill those farmers.
Then he will give
the vineyard to
other farmers.
10 Surely you
have read this
Scripture:[d]

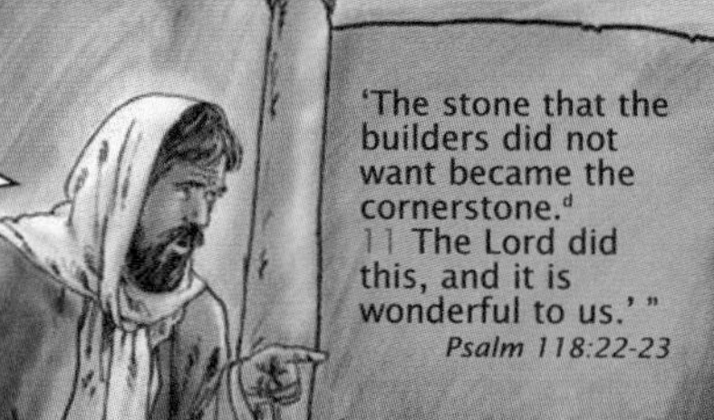
'The stone that the
builders did not
want became the
cornerstone.[d]
11 The Lord did
this, and it is
wonderful to us.' "
Psalm 118:22-23

12 The Jewish
leaders knew that
the story was
about them. So
they wanted to
find a way to
arrest Jesus, but
they were afraid of
the people. So the
leaders left him
and went away.

The Leaders Try to Trap Jesus

13 Later, the Jewish leaders sent some
Pharisees[d] and some men from the group
called Herodians[n] to Jesus. They wanted
to catch Jesus saying something wrong.
14 They came to him and said,

"Teacher, we know that you are
an honest man. You are not afraid of
what other people think about you.
All men are the same to you. And you
teach the truth about God's way. Tell
us: Is it right to pay taxes to Caesar?[d]
Should we pay them, or not?"

15 But Jesus knew what these men
were really trying to do. He said,

"Why are you trying to trap me?
Bring me a silver coin. Let me see it."

16 They gave Jesus a
coin, and he asked,

"Whose picture is on
the coin? And whose
name is written on it?"

12:13 Herodians A political group that followed Herod and his family.

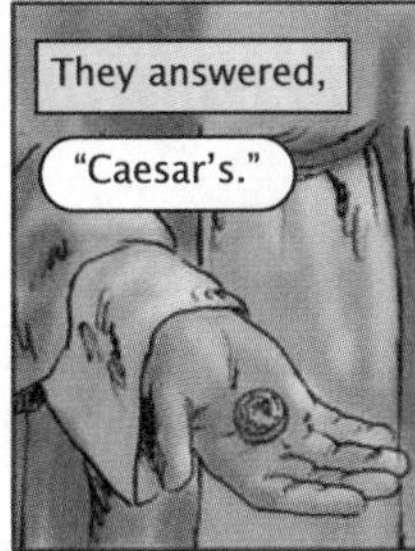
They answered,
"Caesar's."

17 Then Jesus said to them,
"Give to Caesar the things that are Caesar's. And give to God the things that are God's."
The men were amazed at what Jesus said.

Sadducees Try to Trick Jesus

18 Then some Sadducees[d] came
to Jesus. (Sadducees believe that
no person will rise from death.)

The Sadducees asked
Jesus a question.
19 They said,
"Teacher, Moses wrote
that a man's brother might
die. He leaves a wife but no
children. Then that man
must marry the widow and
have children for the dead
brother. 20 There were
seven brothers. The first
brother married but died.
He had no children. 21 So
the second brother married
the widow. But he also died
and had no children. The
same thing happened with
the third brother. 22 All
seven brothers married her
and died. None of the
brothers had any children.
The woman was last to die.
23 But all seven brothers
had married her. So at the
time people rise from
death, whose wife will the
woman be?"
24 Jesus answered,
"Why did you make
this mistake? Is it
because you don't know
what the Scriptures[d] say?
Or is it because you
don't know about the
power of God? 25 When
people rise from death,
there will be no mar-
riage. People will not be
married to each other
but will be like angels in
heaven. 26 Surely you
have read what God said
about people rising from
death. In the book in
which Moses wrote
about the burning bush,[n]
it says that God told
Moses this: 'I am the
God of Abraham, the
God of Isaac, and the
God of Jacob.'[n] 27 God is
the God of living people,
not dead people. You
Sadducees are wrong!"

The Most Important Command

28 One of the teachers
of the law came to Jesus.
He heard Jesus arguing
with the Sadducees[d] and
the Pharisees.[d] He saw
that Jesus gave good
answers to their ques-
tions. So he asked Jesus,

"Which of the commands is most important?"

29 Jesus answered,

"The most im-
portant command
is this: 'Listen,
people of Israel! The
Lord our God, he is
the only Lord.
30 Love the Lord
your God. Love him
with all your heart,
all your soul, all
your mind, and all
your strength.'[n]

12:26 burning bush Read Exodus 3:1-12 in the Old Testament.
12:26 'I am . . . Jacob.' Quotation from Exodus 3:6.
12:29-30 'Listen . . . strength.' Quotation from Deuteronomy 6:4-5.

31 "The second most important command is this: 'Love your neighbor as you love yourself.'[n] These two commands are the most important commands."

32 The man answered,
"That was a good answer, Teacher. You were right when you said these things. God is the only Lord, and there is no other God besides him. 33 One must love God with all his heart, all his mind, and all his strength. And one must love his neighbor as he loves himself. These commands are more important than all the animals and sacrifices we offer to God."

34 Jesus saw that the man answered him wisely. So Jesus said to him,

"You are close to the kingdom of God."

And after that, no one was brave enough to ask Jesus any more questions.
35 Jesus was teaching in the Temple.[d] He asked,
"Why do the teachers of the law say that the Christ[d] is the son of David?

36 David himself, speaking by the Holy Spirit,[d] said:
'The Lord said to my Lord: Sit by me at my right side, until I put your enemies under your control.'
Psalm 110:1
37 David himself calls the Christ 'Lord.' So how can the Christ be David's son?"

The large crowd listened to Jesus with pleasure.

38 Jesus continued teaching. He said,
"Beware of the teachers of the law. They like to walk around wearing clothes that look important. And they love for people to show respect to them in the marketplaces. 39 They love to have the most important seats in the synagogues.[d] And they love to have the most important seats at the feasts. 40 They cheat widows and steal their homes. Then they try to make themselves look good by saying long prayers. God will punish these people terribly."

12:31 'Love . . . yourself.' Quotation from Leviticus 19:18.

True Giving

41 Jesus sat near the Temple[d] money box where people put their gifts. He watched the people put in their money. Many rich people gave large sums of money. 42 Then a poor widow came and gave two very small copper coins. These coins were not worth even a penny.

43 Jesus called his followers to him. He said,

"I tell you the truth. This poor widow gave only two small coins. But she really gave more than all those rich people. 44 The rich have plenty; they gave only what they did not need. This woman is very poor. But she gave all she had. And she needed that money to help her live."

Chapter 13

The Temple Will Be Destroyed

1 Jesus was leaving the Temple.[d] One of his followers said to him,

"Look, Teacher! This Temple has beautiful buildings with very big stones."

2 Jesus said,

"Do you see all these great buildings? Every stone will be thrown to the ground. Not one stone will be left on another."

3 Later, Jesus was sitting on the Mount of Olives.[d] He was alone with Peter, James, John, and Andrew. They could all see the Temple. They asked Jesus,

4 "Tell us, when will all these things happen? And what will show us that the time has come for them to happen?"

5 Jesus said to them:

"Be careful that no one
fools you. 6 Many people will
come and use my name.
They will say, 'I am the One.'
And they will fool many.
7 You will hear about wars
and stories of wars that are
coming. But don't be afraid.
These things must happen
before the end comes.
8 Nations will fight against
other nations. Kingdoms will
fight against other king-
doms. There will be times
when there is no food for
people to eat. And there will
be earthquakes in different
places. These things are like
the first pains when something new is about to be
born.
9 "You must be careful.
People will arrest you and
take you to court. They will
beat you in their syna-
gogues.[d] You will be forced
to stand before kings and
governors, to tell them about
me. This will happen to you
because you follow me.
10 But before these things
happen, the Good News[d]
must be told to all people.
11 When you are arrested
and judged, don't worry
about what you should say.
Say the things God gives you
to say at that time. It will not
really be you speaking. It will
be the Holy Spirit.[d]
12 "Brothers will turn against
their own brothers and give
them over to be killed.
Fathers will turn against
their own children and give
them over to be killed.
Children will fight against
their own parents and cause
their parents to be killed.
13 All people will hate you
because you follow me. But
the person who continues to
be strong until the end will
be saved.
14 "You will see 'the horrible
thing that destroys.'[n] You will
see this thing standing in the
place where it should not
be." (You who read this
should understand what it
means.) "At that time, the
people in Judea should run
away to the mountains. 15 If
a person is on the roof[n] of
his house, he must not go
down to take anything out of
his house. 16 If a person is
in the field, he must not go
back to get his coat. 17 At
that time, it will be hard for
women who are pregnant or
have nursing babies. 18 Pray
that these things will not
happen in winter. 19 This is
because those days will be
full of trouble. There will be
more trouble than there has
ever been since the beginning, when God made the
world. And nothing as bad
will ever happen again.
20 God has decided to make
that terrible time short. If
that time were not made
short, then no one would go
on living. But God will make
that time short to help his
special people whom he has
chosen.

13:14 'the horrible . . . destroys.' Mentioned in Daniel 9:27; 12:11 (cf. Daniel 11:31).
13:15 roof In Bible times houses were built with flat roofs. The roof was used for drying things such as flax and fruit. And it was used as an extra room, as a place for worship and as a place to sleep in the summer.

21 "At that time, some-
one might say to you,
'Look, there is the Christ!'[d]
Or another person might
say, 'There he is!' But don't
believe them. 22 False
Christs and false prophets[d]
will come and perform great
wonders and miracles.[d] They
will do these things to the
people God has chosen.
They will do these things to
try to fool them, if that is
possible. 23 So be careful.
For I have warned you about
all this before it happens.
24 "During the days after
this trouble comes,

> 'The sun will grow dark.
> And the moon will not
> give its light. 25 The
> stars will fall from the
> sky. And everything in
> the sky will be changed.'
> *Isaiah 13:10; 34:4*

26 "Then people will see
the Son of Man[d] coming in
clouds with great power and
glory. 27 The Son of Man
will send his angels all
around the earth. They will
gather his chosen people
from every part of the earth.
28 "The fig tree teaches us
a lesson: When its branches
become green and soft, and
new leaves begin to grow,
then you know that summer
is near. 29 So also when
you see all these things
happening, then you will
know that the time is near,
ready to come. 30 I tell you
the truth. All these things
will happen while the people of this time are still living. 31 The whole world,
earth and sky, will be
destroyed, but the words I
have said will never be
destroyed.
32 "No one knows when
that day or time will be. The
Son and the angels in heav-
en don't know. Only the
Father knows. 33 Be careful!
Always be ready![n] You don't
know when that time will
be. 34 It is like a man who
goes on a trip. He leaves his
house and lets his servants
take care of it. He gives
each servant a special job to
do. One servant has the
work of guarding the door.
The man tells this servant
always to be watchful. This
is what I am now telling
you. 35 You must always be
ready. You don't know when
the owner of the house will
come back. He might come
in the evening, or at mid-
night, or in the early morning, or when the sun rises.
36 He might come back
quickly. If you are always
ready, then he will not find
you sleeping. 37 I tell you
this, and I say this to everyone: 'Be ready!' "

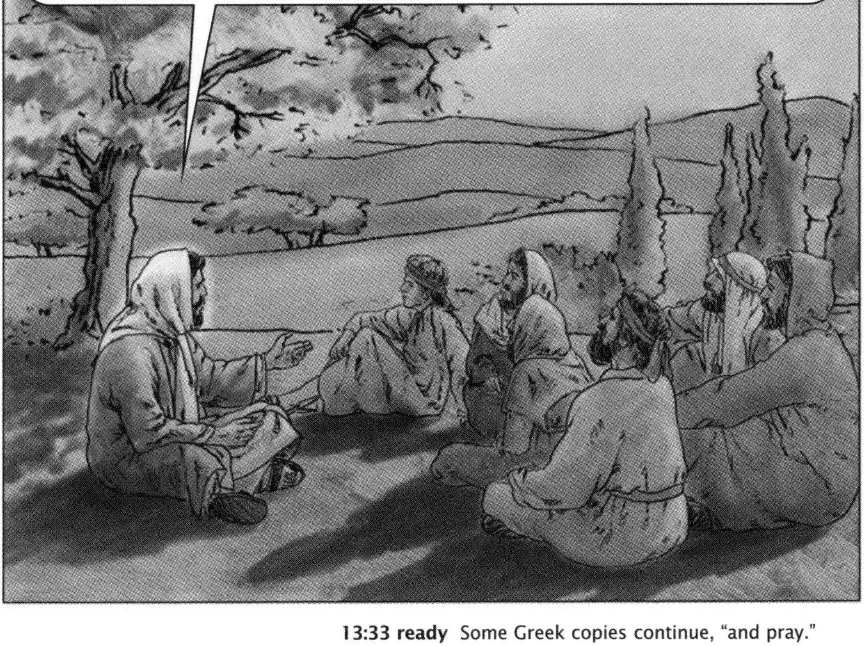

13:33 ready Some Greek copies continue, "and pray."

Chapter
14
The Plan to Kill Jesus

1 It was now only two days before the Passover[d] and the Feast[d] of Unleavened Bread. The leading priests and teachers of the law were trying to find a way to use some trick to arrest Jesus and kill him. 2 But they said,
"We must not do it during the feast. The people might cause a riot."

A Woman with Perfume for Jesus
3 Jesus was in Bethany. He was at dinner in the house of Simon, who had a harmful skin disease. While Jesus was there, a woman came to him. She had an alabaster[d] jar filled with very expensive perfume, made of pure nard.[d] The woman opened the jar and poured the perfume on Jesus' head.

4 Some of those who were there saw this and became angry. They complained to each other, saying,

"Why waste that perfume? 5 It was worth a full year's work. It could be sold, and the money could be given to the poor."

They spoke to the woman sharply.

6 Jesus said,
"Don't bother the woman. Why are you troubling her? She did a beautiful thing for me.

7 You will always have the poor with you. You can help them anytime you want. But you will not always have me.

8 This woman did the only thing she could do for me. She poured perfume on my body. She did this before I die to prepare me for burial.

9 I tell you the truth. The Good News[d] will be told to people in all the world. And in every place it is preached, what this woman has done will be told. And people will remember her."

Judas Becomes an Enemy of Jesus

10 One of the 12 followers, Judas Iscariot, went to talk to the leading priests. Judas offered to give Jesus to them.
11 The leading priests were pleased about this. They promised to pay Judas money. So he waited for the best time to give Jesus to them.

Jesus Eats the Passover Feast

12 It was now the first day of the Feast[d] of Unleavened Bread. This was a time when the Jews always sacrificed the Passover[d] lambs. Jesus' followers came to him. They said,

"We will go and prepare everything for the Passover Feast. Where do you want to eat the feast?"

13 Jesus sent two of his followers and said to them,

"Go into the city. A man carrying a jar of water will meet you. Follow him.
14 He will go into a house. Tell the owner of the house, 'The Teacher asks that you show us the room where he and his followers can eat the Passover Feast.'

15 The owner will show you a large room upstairs. This room is ready. Prepare the food for us there."

16 So the followers left and went into the city. Everything happened as Jesus had said. So they prepared the Passover Feast.
17 In the evening, Jesus went to that house with the 12.

18 While they were all eating, Jesus said,

"I tell you the truth. One of you will give me to my enemies—one of you eating with me now."

19 The followers were very sad to hear this. Each one said to Jesus,
"I am not the one, am I?"
20 Jesus answered,
"The man who is against me is 1 of the 12. He is the one who dips his bread into the bowl with me.

21 The Son of Man[d] must go and die. The Scriptures[d] say this will happen. But how terrible it will be for the person who gives the Son of Man to be killed. It would be better for that person if he had never been born."

The Lord's Supper

22 While they were eating, Jesus took some bread. He thanked God for it

and broke it. Then he gave it to his followers and said,

"Take it. This bread is my body."

23 Then Jesus took a cup. He thanked God for it and gave it to the followers. All the followers drank from the cup.
24 Then Jesus said,
"This is my blood which begins the new[n] agreement that God makes with his people. This blood is poured out for many.
25 I tell you the truth. I will not drink of this fruit of the vine[n] again until that day when I drink it new in the kingdom of God."

26 They sang a hymn and went out to the Mount of Olives.[d]

Jesus' Followers Will All Leave Him

27 Then Jesus told the followers,

"You will all lose your faith in me. It is written in the Scriptures:

'I will kill the shepherd,
and the sheep will scatter.'
Zechariah 13:7

28 But after I rise from death, I will go ahead of you into Galilee."

29 Peter said,
"All the other followers may lose their faith. But I will not."

14:24 new Some Greek copies do not have this word. Compare Luke 22:20.
14:25 fruit of the vine Product of the grapevine; this may also be translated "wine."

30 Jesus answered,
"I tell you the truth. Tonight you will say you don't know me. You will say this three times before the rooster crows twice."
31 But Peter answered strongly,
"I will never say that I don't know you! I will even die with you!"
And all the other followers said the same thing.

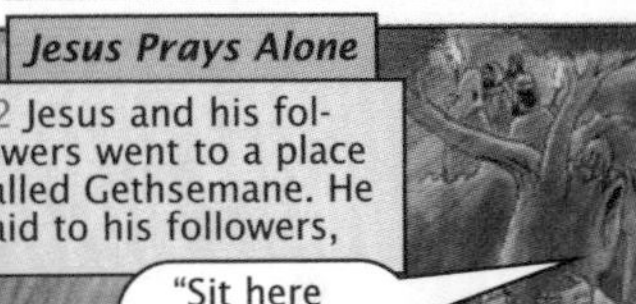
Jesus Prays Alone
32 Jesus and his followers went to a place called Gethsemane. He said to his followers,

"Sit here while I pray."
33 Jesus told Peter, James, and John to come with him. Then Jesus began to be very sad and troubled.

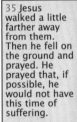

34 He said to them,
"I am full of sorrow. My heart is breaking with sadness.

Stay here and watch."

35 Jesus walked a little farther away from them. Then he fell on the ground and prayed. He prayed that, if possible, he would not have this time of suffering.

36 He prayed,
"Abba,[n] Father! You can do all things. Let me not have this cup[n] of suffering.

But do what you want, not what I want."

37 Then Jesus went back to his followers. He found them asleep. He said to Peter,
"Simon, why are you sleeping? You could not stay awake with me for one hour?

14:36 Abba Name that a child called his father. **14:36 cup** Jesus is talking about the bad things that will happen to him. Accepting these things will be very hard, like drinking a cup of something that tastes very bitter.

38 "Stay awake and pray that you will not be tempted. Your spirit wants to do what is right, but your body is weak."

39 Again Jesus went away and prayed the same thing. 40 Then he went back to the followers. Again he found them asleep because their eyes were very heavy. And they did not know what to say to Jesus. 41 After Jesus prayed a third time, he went back to his followers. He said to them,

"You are still sleeping and resting? That's enough! The time has come for the Son of Man[d] to be given to sinful people.

42 Get up! We must go. Here comes the man who has turned against me."

Jesus Is Arrested

43 While Jesus was still speaking, Judas came up. Judas was 1 of the 12 followers. He had many people with him. They were sent from the leading priests, the teachers of the law, and the Jewish elders. Those with Judas had swords and clubs. 44 Judas had planned a signal for them. He had said,

"The man I kiss is Jesus. Arrest him and guard him while you lead him away."

45 So Judas went to Jesus and said,

"Teacher!"

and kissed him.

46 Then the men grabbed Jesus and arrested him.

47 One of the followers standing near drew his sword. He struck the servant of the high priest with the sword and cut off his ear.

48 Then Jesus said,

"You came to get me with swords and clubs as if I were a criminal. 49 Every day I was with you teaching in the Temple.[d] You did not arrest me there. But all these things have happened to make the Scriptures[d] come true."

50 Then all of Jesus' followers left him and ran away.

51 A young man, wearing only a linen cloth, was following Jesus. The people also grabbed him. 52 But the cloth he was wearing came off, and he ran away naked.

Jesus Before the Leaders

53 The people who arrested Jesus led him to the house of the high priest. All the leading priests, the Jewish elders, and the teachers of the law were gathered there.

54 Peter followed far behind and entered the courtyard of the high priest's house. There he sat with the guards, warming himself by the fire.

55 The leading priests and all the Jewish council tried to find something that Jesus had done wrong so they could kill him. But the council could find no proof against him. 56 Many people came and told false things about him. But all said different things—none of them agreed.
57 Then some men stood up and lied about Jesus. They said,

58 "We heard this man say, 'I will destroy this Temple[d] that men made. And three days later, I will build another Temple—a Temple not made by men.' "

59 But even the things these men said did not agree.
60 Then the high priest stood before them and said to Jesus,

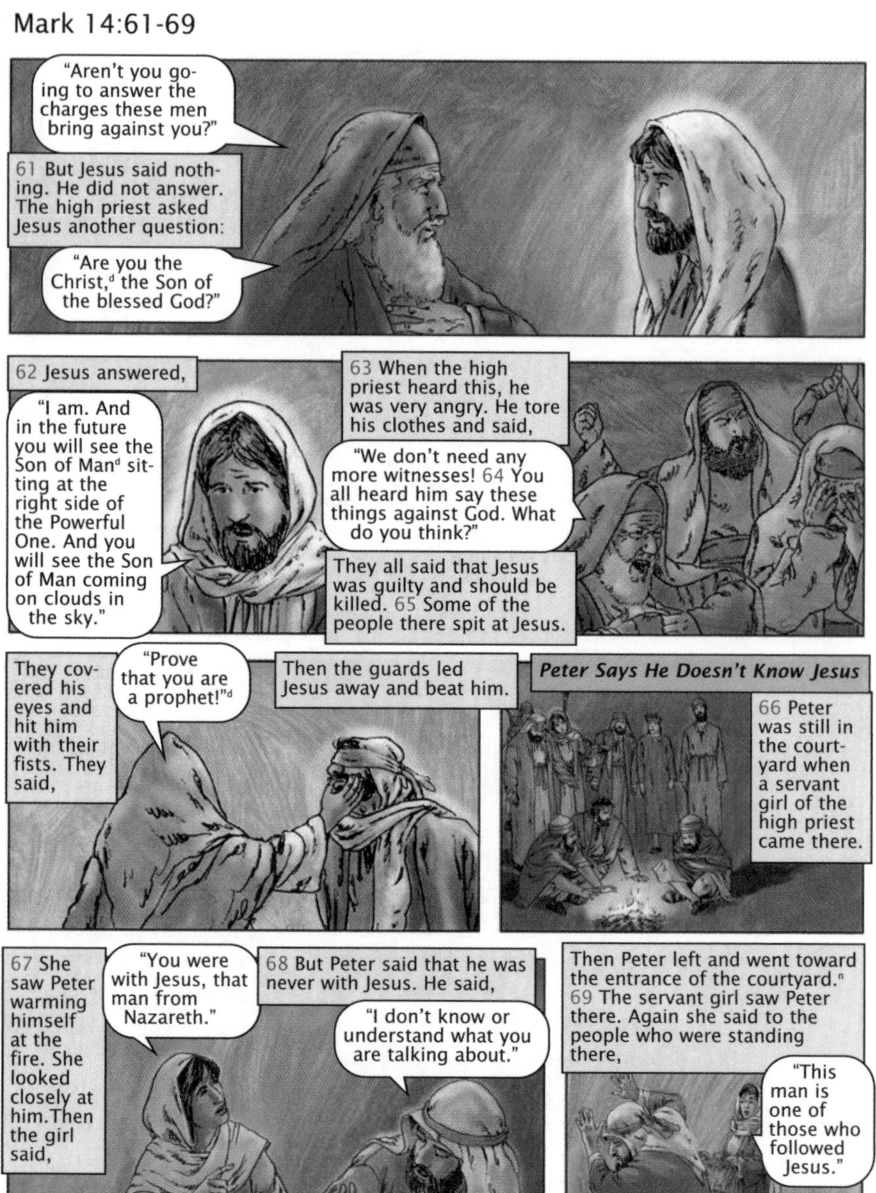
"Aren't you going to answer the charges these men bring against you?"
61 But Jesus said nothing. He did not answer. The high priest asked Jesus another question:
"Are you the Christ,[d] the Son of the blessed God?"
62 Jesus answered,
"I am. And in the future you will see the Son of Man[d] sitting at the right side of the Powerful One. And you will see the Son of Man coming on clouds in the sky."
63 When the high priest heard this, he was very angry. He tore his clothes and said,
"We don't need any more witnesses! 64 You all heard him say these things against God. What do you think?"
They all said that Jesus was guilty and should be killed. 65 Some of the people there spit at Jesus.
They covered his eyes and hit him with their fists. They said,
"Prove that you are a prophet!"[d]
Then the guards led Jesus away and beat him.
Peter Says He Doesn't Know Jesus
66 Peter was still in the courtyard when a servant girl of the high priest came there.
67 She saw Peter warming himself at the fire. She looked closely at him.Then the girl said,
"You were with Jesus, that man from Nazareth."
68 But Peter said that he was never with Jesus. He said,
"I don't know or understand what you are talking about."
Then Peter left and went toward the entrance of the courtyard.[n] 69 The servant girl saw Peter there. Again she said to the people who were standing there,
"This man is one of those who followed Jesus."

14:68 Verse 68 Many Greek copies add: "And the rooster crowed."

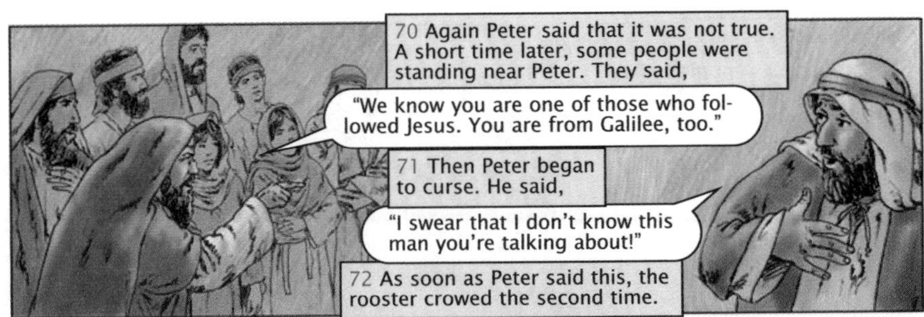
70 Again Peter said that it was not true. A short time later, some people were standing near Peter. They said,
"We know you are one of those who followed Jesus. You are from Galilee, too."
71 Then Peter began to curse. He said,
"I swear that I don't know this man you're talking about!"
72 As soon as Peter said this, the rooster crowed the second time.

Then Peter remembered what Jesus had told him:
"Before the rooster crows twice, you will say three times that you don't know me."
Then Peter was very sad and began to cry.

Chapter 15

Pilate Questions Jesus

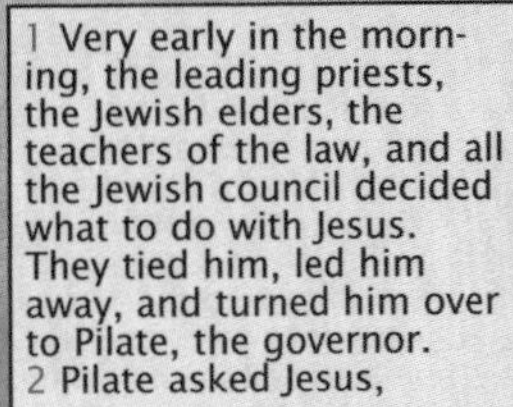
1 Very early in the morning, the leading priests, the Jewish elders, the teachers of the law, and all the Jewish council decided what to do with Jesus. They tied him, led him away, and turned him over to Pilate, the governor.
2 Pilate asked Jesus,

"Are you the king of the Jews?"
Jesus answered,
"Yes, I am."

Pilate Tries to Free Jesus

3 The leading priests accused Jesus of many things. 4 So Pilate asked Jesus another question. He said,
"You can see that these people are accusing you of many things. Why don't you answer?"
5 But Jesus still said nothing. Pilate was very surprised at this.
6 Every year at the Passover[d] time the governor would free one person from prison. He would free any person the people wanted him to free.
7 At that time, there was a man named Barabbas in prison. He was a rebel and had committed murder during a riot. 8 The crowd came to Pilate and asked him to free a prisoner as he always did.

9 Pilate asked them,

"Do you want me to free the king of the Jews?"

10 Pilate knew that the
leading priests had given
Jesus to him because they
were jealous of Jesus.
11 And the leading
priests had persuaded the
people to ask Pilate to
free Barabbas, not Jesus.
12 Pilate asked the crowd
again,

"So what should I do with this man you call the king of the Jews?"

13 They shouted,

"Kill him on a cross!"

14 Pilate asked,

"Why? What wrong has he done?"

But they shouted louder and louder,

"Kill him on a cross!"

15 Pilate wanted to
please the crowd. So he
freed Barabbas for them.
And Pilate told the
soldiers to beat Jesus
with whips. Then he gave
Jesus to the soldiers to
be killed on a cross.
16 Pilate's soldiers took
Jesus into the governor's
palace (called the Praeto-
rium). They called all the
other soldiers together.

17 They put a purple
robe on Jesus. Then they
used thorny branches to
make a crown. They put
it on his head. 18 Then
they called out to him,

"Hail, King of the Jews!"

19 The soldiers beat Jesus
on the head many times
with a stick. They also spit
on him. Then they made fun
of him by bowing on their
knees and worshiping him.

20 After they finished making
fun of him, the soldiers took
off the purple robe and put
his own clothes on him again.
Then they led Jesus out of the
palace to be killed on a cross.

Jesus Is Killed on a Cross

21 There was a man from Cyrene
coming from the fields to the
city. The man was Simon, the
father of Alexander and Rufus.
The soldiers forced Simon to
carry the cross for Jesus.

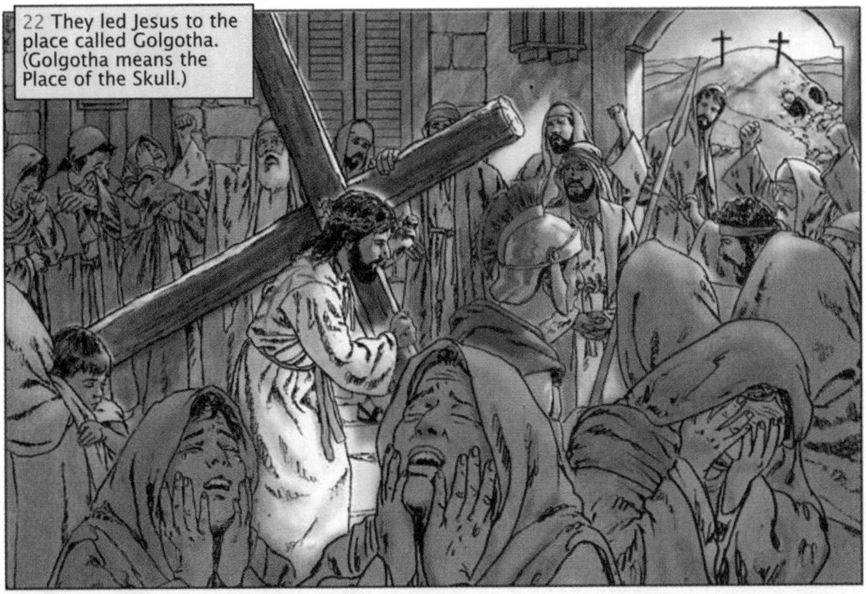

22 They led Jesus to the
place called Golgotha.
(Golgotha means the
Place of the Skull.)

23 At Golgotha the soldiers
tried to give Jesus wine to
drink. This wine was mixed
with myrrh.[d] But he refused
to drink it. 24 The soldiers
nailed Jesus to a cross.

Then they
divided his
clothes among
themselves.
They threw
lots[d] to decide
which clothes
each soldier
would get.

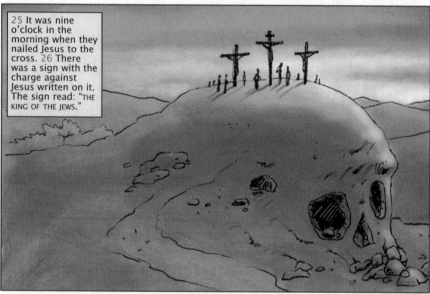

25 It was nine
o'clock in the
morning when they
nailed Jesus to the
cross. 26 There
was a sign with the
charge against
Jesus written on it.
The sign read: "THE
KING OF THE JEWS."

27 They also put
two robbers on
crosses beside
Jesus, one on the
right, and the
other on the left.
28 [And the
Scripture came
true that says,
"They put him
with criminals."] [n]

15:28 And . . . criminals. Some Greek copies do not contain the bracketed text which quotes from Isaiah 53:12.

29 People walked by and insulted Jesus. They shook their heads, saying,
"You said you could destroy the Temple[d] and build it again in three days. 30 So save yourself! Come down from that cross!"
31 The leading priests and the teachers of the law were also there. They made fun of Jesus just as the other people did.
They said among themselves,
"He saved other people, but he can't save himself. 32 If he is really the Christ,[d] the king of Israel, then let him come down from the cross now. We will see this, and then we will believe in him."
The robbers who were being killed on the crosses beside Jesus also insulted him.

Jesus Dies

33 At noon the whole country became dark. This darkness lasted for three hours. 34 At three o'clock Jesus cried in a loud voice,
"Eloi, Eloi, lama sabachthani."
This means,
"My God, my God, why have you left me alone?"

35 Some of the people standing there heard this. They said,
"Listen! He is calling Elijah."

36 One man there ran and got a sponge. He filled the sponge with vinegar and tied it to a stick. Then he used the stick to give the sponge to Jesus to drink from it. The man said,
"We should wait now and see if Elijah will come to take him down from the cross."

37 Then Jesus cried in a loud voice and died.

38 When Jesus died, the curtain in the Temple[n] split into two pieces. The tear started at the top and tore all the way to the bottom.

39 The army officer that was standing there before the cross saw what happened when Jesus died.[n] The officer said,

"This man really was the Son of God!"

40 Some women were standing at a distance from the cross, watching.

15:38 curtain in the Temple A curtain divided the Most Holy Place from the other part of the Temple. That was the special building in Jerusalem where God commanded the Jews to worship him. **15:39 when Jesus died** Some Greek copies read "when Jesus cried out and died."

Some of these women
were Mary Magdalene,
Salome, and Mary the
mother of James and
Joseph. (James was her
youngest son.) 41 These
were the women who
followed Jesus in Galilee
and cared for him. Many
other women were also
there who had come
with Jesus to Jerusalem.

Jesus Is Buried

42 This was Preparation[d]
Day. (That means the day
before the Sabbath[d] day.) It
was becoming dark. 43 A
man named Joseph from Ari-
mathea was brave enough to
go to Pilate and ask for
Jesus' body. Joseph was an
important member of the
Jewish council. He was one of
the people who wanted the
kingdom of God to come.

44 Pilate wondered if Jesus
was already dead. Pilate
called the army officer
who guarded Jesus and
asked him if Jesus had
already died. 45 The officer told Pilate that he was
dead. So Pilate told Joseph
he could have the body.
46 Joseph bought some
linen cloth, took the body
down from the cross and
wrapped it in the linen.

He put the body in
a tomb that was
cut in a wall of
rock. Then he
closed the tomb by
rolling a very large
stone to cover the
entrance. 47 And
Mary Magdalene
and Mary the
mother of Joseph
saw the place
where Jesus was
laid.

Chapter 16

Jesus Rises from Death

1 The day after the
Sabbath[d] day, Mary
Magdalene, Mary the
mother of James, and
Salome bought some
sweet-smelling spices
to put on Jesus' body.
2 Very early on that
day, the first day of
the week, the women
were on their way to
the tomb. It was soon
after sunrise. 3 They
said to each other,

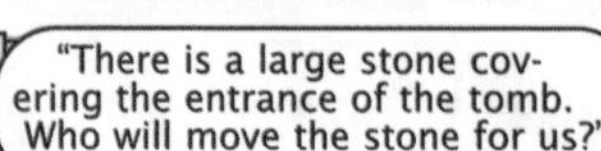
"There is a large stone cov-
ering the entrance of the tomb.
Who will move the stone for us?"

4 Then the women looked
and saw that the stone was
already moved. The stone was
very large, but it was moved
away from the entrance.

5 The women entered the tomb and saw a
young man wearing a white robe. He was sitting
on the right side, and the women were afraid.
6 But the man said,

"Don't be
afraid. You are look-
ing for Jesus from
Nazareth, the one
who was killed on a
cross. He has risen
from death. He is
not here. Look, here
is the place they laid
him. 7 Now go and
tell his followers
and Peter, 'Jesus is
going into Galilee.
He will be there
before you. You will
see him there as he
told you before.' "

8 The women were confused
and shaking with fear. They
left the tomb and ran away.
They did not tell anyone
about what happened,
because they were afraid.[n]

Some Followers See Jesus

9 Jesus rose
from death
early on the
first day of the
week. He
showed himself
first to Mary
Magdalene.
One time in the
past, he had
forced seven
demons[d] to
leave Mary.

10 After Mary
saw Jesus, she
went and told
his followers.
They were very
sad and were
crying. 11 But
Mary told them
that Jesus was
alive. She said
that she had
seen him, but
the followers did
not believe her.

12 Later,
Jesus
showed
himself to
two of his
followers
while they
were walk-
ing in the
country. But
Jesus did
not look the
same as
before.

13 These followers went back to the others and told them what had happened.
Again, the followers did not believe them.

16:8 Verse 8 Some early Greek copies end the book with verse 8.

Jesus Talks to the Apostles

14 Later Jesus showed
himself to the 11 fol-
lowers while they were
eating. He criticized
them because they had
little faith. They were
stubborn and refused
to believe those who
had seen him after he
had risen from death.

15 Jesus said to the followers,

"Go everywhere in the
world. Tell the Good
News[d] to everyone.
16 Anyone who believes
and is baptized will be
saved. But he who does
not believe will be
judged guilty. 17 And
those who believe will be
able to do these things as
proof: They will use my
name to force demons[d]
out of people. They will
speak in languages they
never learned. 18 They
will pick up snakes with-
out being hurt. And they
will drink poison without
being hurt. They will
touch the sick, and the
sick will be healed."

19 After the Lord Jesus
said these things to the
followers, he was car-
ried up into heaven.
There, Jesus sat at the
right side of God.
20 The followers went
everywhere in the
world and told the
Good News to people.
And the Lord helped
them. The Lord proved
that the Good News
they told was true by
giving them power to
work miracles.[d]